Heaven Made Real

The Best Is Yet to Come

Heaven Made Real

The Best Is Yet to Come

Dr. Tim Sheets

 Unless otherwise identified, Scripture quotations are from the King James Version of the Bible. Also quoted are the Amplified Bible (AMP): Amplified New Testament © 1954, 1958, 1987 by The Lockman Foundation; Old Testament © 1965, 1987 by The Zondervan Corporation; and The New Testament in the Translation of Monsignor Ronald Knox © 1944 by Sheed and Ward, Inc.

Take note that the name satan and related names are not capitalized. We choose not to acknowledge him, even to the point of violating grammatical rules.

Treasure House

An Imprint of

Destiny Image® Publishers, Inc.

P.O. Box 310

Shippensburg, PA 17257-0310

"For where your treasure is
there will your heart be also." Matthew 6:21

ISBN 1-56043-276-4

For Worldwide Distribution

Printed in the U.S.A.

Treasure House books are available through these fine distributors outside the United States:

Christian Growth, Inc.
Jalan Kilang-Timor, Singapore 0315

Omega Distributors
Ponsonby, Auckland, New Zealand

Rhema Ministries Trading
Randburg, Rep. of South Africa

Salvation Book Centre
Petaling, Jaya, Malaysia

Successful Christian Living
Capetown, Rep. of South Africa

Vine Christian Centre
Mid Glamorgan, Wales, United Kingdom

WA Buchanan Company
Geebung, Queensland, Australia

Word Alive
Niverville, Manitoba, Canada

This book and all other Destiny Image
and Treasure House books
are available at Christian bookstores everywhere.

Call for a bookstore nearest you.
1-800-722-6774
Or reach us on the Internet: **http://www.reapernet.com**

Contents

	"Is the Bible True?"	ix
Chapter 1	A Model on Earth	1
Chapter 2	Heaven Is a Real Place	17
Chapter 3	Locating Heaven	31
Chapter 4	Your Glorified Body	41
Chapter 5	Your Proper Self	53
Chapter 6	The Appearance of God and Angels	67
Chapter 7	Eternal Things	85
Chapter 8	The Great Cloud of Witnesses	101
Chapter 9	Babies, Children, and Heaven	113
Chapter 10	The City of God	127
Chapter 11	More of the New Jerusalem	143
Chapter 12	The Final Ages Begin	153
Chapter 13	Life on the New Earth	169
Chapter 14	Rewards and Seeing Jesus as He Is	185
Appendix	People's Experiences of Heaven	201

“Is the Bible True?”

You may not believe the Bible is proof of anything if men wrote it. But consider this: If God *is* God, isn’t He big enough to get His point across, whether He has to use men or donkeys?

If the Bible, or Word of God, has no merit, if there is not something real and alive about it, then why does even the presence of a Bible evoke some sort of passionate response in most anyone?

Whatever your inclination, do yourself a favor and take a look at this book. Note the context of the Scripture passages outlined. See if the Word of God doesn’t come alive for you...and if something deep inside you doesn’t say, “Thank God, it *is* true!”

Chapter 1

A Model on Earth

There must be something more to Heaven if the apostle Paul preferred it to life on earth:

For to me...to die is gain.

...to be with Christ...is far better.

Philippians 1:21,23

Yet most people think of Heaven as some kind of "old folks home." They view Heaven as nothing better than a glorified retirement village where you go when you've exhausted everything good in life, or when you get in somebody's way. You play harps and sing, but life there becomes a poor second to this world with its riches, glamour, and vitality.

Nothing could be farther from the truth. It is time for the truth to be told. It is time for Heaven to be made real—not from someone else's story of a near-death experience or of somebody's dream—but straight from the truth in the Word of God!

A Better Place

Most of us miss the significance of one of the greatest passages of Scripture that describe Heaven:

By faith Abraham, when he was called to go out into a place which he should after receive for an inheritance, obeyed; and he went out, not knowing whither he went.

By faith he sojourned in the land of promise, as in a strange country, dwelling in tabernacles with Isaac and Jacob, the heirs with him of the same promise:

For he looked for ***a city which hath foundations, whose builder and maker is God.***

Through faith also Sara herself received strength to conceive seed, and was delivered of a child when she was past age, because she judged Him faithful who had promised.

Therefore sprang there even of one, and him as good as dead, so many as the stars of the sky in multitude, and as the sand which is by the sea shore innumerable.

These all died in faith, ***not having received the promises, but having seen them afar off, and were persuaded of them, and embraced them, and confessed that they were strangers and pilgrims on the earth.***

For they that say such things declare plainly that they seek a country.

And truly, if they had been mindful of that country from whence they came out, they might have had opportunity to have returned.

But now they desire a ***better country, that is, an heavenly****: wherefore God is not ashamed to be called their God:* ***for He hath prepared for them a city****.*

Hebrews 11:8-16

We most often think of these verses as a tremendous inspiration for faith as we review the sacrifices our forefathers made to believe God.

Yet we need to understand another purpose to these Scriptures. This purpose is to show that our faith has an object—and that object is the *reward of a real place called Heaven*! This earth is not our final home!

That means the ultimate goal of our life is gaining Heaven. The end purpose of our faith is to reach Heaven, the eternal City of God!

Thank God for faith that enables us to live now. Thank God for the stories of those men and women of faith who overcame all odds in this life. Yet the consummate reason for our faith is not to obtain any praise or gain this world can offer. It's not to acquire wealth or even health, though we can and should believe for these things.

The consummate purpose for our faith is to grant us access to a better place, a heavenly country. It's to open to us an eternal home, the gift of a Savior who sacrificed His very life that we might obtain it.

A More Enduring Substance

The apostle Paul (whom I believe wrote the Book of Hebrews) carefully addressed that passage of Scripture to the Hebrews or Jewish people of his day.

Those people highly celebrated earthly Jerusalem as their symbol of hope. That city was their bastion of peace, the "great city" of David; their "mecca," if you will. Yet Paul told them to aim their faith higher, to a new Jerusalem—a city whose builder and maker is God.

In that city, nothing ever fades. That city's reward and promise last forever. Paul knew that nothing you could suffer or lose on this earth would ever compare with what you will receive:

> *For ye had compassion of me in my bonds, and took joyfully the spoiling of your goods, knowing in yourselves that ye have in heaven a better and an enduring substance.*
>
> Hebrews 10:34

Other Bible translations are even clearer. Weymouth's translation says that in Heaven you will have "more valuable possessions that will remain." The Basic English New Testament says, "better property—that will keep forever."

J.B. Phillips' New Testament says, "a much more solid and lasting treasure." That means you will receive an inheritance that cannot be spoiled; Heaven is a place of enduring substance where your possessions will never be lost or stolen, or suffer decay.

This real promise is very much worth the wait. Paul said:

> *Cast not away therefore your confidence, which hath great recompence of reward.*
>
> *For ye have need of patience, that, after ye have done the will of God, ye might receive the promise.*
>
> *For yet a little while, and He that shall come will come, and will not tarry.*
>
> Hebrews 10:35-37

Paul also knew that if we would grasp the promise and reality of Heaven, it would change the way we live now.

Now the just shall live by faith: but if any man draw back, my soul shall have no pleasure in him.

Hebrews 10:38

Now faith is the **substance** *of things hoped for, the evidence of things not seen.*

Hebrews 11:1

The Greek word for "substance" is *hupostasis*, meaning "support base, title deed, or assurance."

It means that by faith in Jesus Christ, you already have property in Heaven with your name on it. The Lord is your title deed to it! The inheritance you have there is more valuable and lasting than anything you now possess.

The point is that you are only "passing through" this earth as a "stranger" and a "pilgrim" (see Heb. 11:13).

The Greek word for "strangers" is *xenos*, meaning a "foreigner" or "alien" who "makes himself at home." "Pilgrims" are those people who are on "a journey to a better country."

That simply means you are a foreigner on this soil who makes himself at home while on a journey to a better country called Heaven!

"Better" is the Greek word *kreisson*, meaning "superior, more excellent, or more favorable." It literally means "the highest form of excellence."

There's no better description for the superior place for which we are bound—a place Jesus Himself called "the paradise of God" (Rev. 2:7).

A New Perspective

Most likely, Heaven is far different from what you think it is.

It's important to let go of our misconceptions and imaginations. As we continue, we'll see that we won't actually spend all our time floating on a cloud and singing. Nor will we indulge ourselves forever doing what we liked best on earth.

Man's notions of Heaven are pitiful at best, mainly because we don't think or see things the way God does (see Is. 55:8). Heaven is far more glorious, but its only accurate description comes from God's own Word.

The first idea we must dispel is that if you are "heavenly minded, you're no earthly good." This kind of thinking has actually robbed Christians of much of our joy for here and now. We have been shamed away from our hope and from the very things God wants us to think about now to receive courage and endurance. He tells us to "set our mind on things above"! (See Colossians 3:2.)

Actually, the more heavenly minded you are, the more earthly good you can be, provided you understand what Heaven really is. The right beliefs can sustain and guide you through life like a compass does.

How you view Heaven can mean the difference between a frustrating life of running in circles or one that offers true satisfaction and reward!

It's surely worth gaining an accurate perspective.

The Church on Earth

God has put an excellent model of the truth of Heaven right before our eyes. It is the Church on earth!

God intends for the Church, among other things, to model the best of Heaven to mankind *now*, through her example, and thereby draw people to Christ. The most important part of Heaven is its residents and their relationships to God and one another. Such is also the case for the Church on earth.

Literally, "church," or *ekklesia*, means "called-out ones." It is God's people on earth who live for Him. It is not the church building itself, as some may think. In fact, when we get to Heaven, there will be no need for "the Church" as we now know it, or for church buildings. Heaven will be filled with the people of God, and there will be no need for any separate category:

> *And I saw no temple therein: for the Lord God Almighty and the Lamb are the temple of it.*
>
> Revelation 21:22

Until we get to Heaven, the Church on earth holds an extremely significant position. It provides a tangible meeting place for God and His people, and is the means of sharing the reality of God with the world.

This earthly institution significantly models Heaven in many ways.

Just as we will serve God in Heaven, the same opportunity is extended to us now through the Church. Whether we are ushers, greeters, Sunday school teachers, singers, or preachers, we model to the world this vital aspect of Heaven.

How we model such service to God is crucial. The Church actually reflects the society of Heaven.

The simple fact that millions of people take time to go to church every Sunday sends a message to the world. It says that God is real and worthwhile, and that they can meet with Him now. It says God is relevant to their lives and their families, and that His answers work.

It gives the world a witness of Heaven that it cannot deny.

This is not to discount the one-on-one relationship and time we spend with Father God alone. That is essential to real faith. Yet it should not take the place of our coming together as His Church and of serving the purposes He has established for all eternity.

Because God has purposed to model Heaven through the Church, we must also remember that "church" is on His terms, not ours. God has called and set each member in the Body as it has pleased Him (see 1 Cor. 12:18). He has formed the *ekklesia*, the "called-out ones." Therefore, it's His mandate and organization, not our option!

Assembling Together

Many people are confused today about the need to attend church. Yet our most crucial gains and growth occur through the vehicle of the Church on earth and the relationships there.

If we truly want to understand the eternal nature of Christ, we must be attached to Jesus, the Head of the Church. However, it is impossible to have a relationship with a head unless it is attached to a body. In this case, it is the Body of

Christ (see Eph. 5:23). Quite simply, the Body is members coming together (see 1 Cor. 12:20). All true-life transmissions require the joining of the two!

Scripture makes it very plain:

And let us consider one another to provoke unto love and to good works:

Not forsaking the assembling of ourselves together, as the manner of some is; but exhorting one another: and so much the more, as ye see the day approaching.

Hebrews 10:24-25

Knox's translation says, "not abandoning our common assemblies." Berkeley's version of the New Testament says, "not neglecting our own church meetings." The New English Bible says, "not staying away from our meetings."

J.B. Phillips' translation says, "Let us not hold aloof from our church meetings." Taylor's translation says, "Assemble together more as you see the day of His coming back drawing near."

This means that if we really believe Jesus is coming back soon, we should be trying to assemble more, not less! When we do so, we model to the world what we really believe: that Heaven is a real place, worth moving toward in our daily life choices; that it is worth far more than the latest network movie or the mall!

Laodicean Mistake

You can be sure that there will be a lot of opposition to keep people from becoming an active part of the local Body of Christ—for our sustenance is to be found there.

Oddly enough, one of the worst enemies of how God intends to model Heaven through the Church is our own sense of self-sufficiency.

We can see that lesson from the Laodicean church of Revelation:

> *I know thy works, that thou art neither cold nor hot: I would thou wert cold or hot.*
>
> *So then because thou art lukewarm, and neither cold nor hot, I will spue thee out of My mouth.*
>
> *Because thou sayest, I am rich, and increased with goods, and have need of nothing; and knowest not that thou art wretched, and miserable, and poor, and blind, and naked:*
>
> *I counsel thee to buy of Me gold tried in the fire, that thou mayest be rich; and white raiment, that thou mayest be clothed, and that the shame of thy nakedness do not appear; and anoint thine eyes with eyesalve, that thou mayest see.*
>
> *As many as I love, I rebuke and chasten: be zealous therefore, and repent.*
>
> *Behold, I stand at the door, and knock: if any man hear My voice, and open the door, I will come in to him, and will sup with him, and he with Me.*
>
> *To him that overcometh will I grant to sit with Me in My throne, even as I also overcame, and am set down with My Father in His throne.*
>
> *He that hath an ear, let him hear what the Spirit saith unto the* ***churches****.*
>
> Revelation 3:15-22

This particular group of believers considered themselves to be very mature. They had no need for church..."You know, we can study on our own; we can study what we want. We pray at home. We can handle it. You see, we're rich and increased with goods. We don't really need anything. Our business is successful, and frankly, we're busy. Church takes time."

But God saw things a little differently, and told the Laodiceans to repent! The purposes of God in the current age are accomplished in the Church. When God has something to say, He tells it to the Church through the churches (see Rev. 3:22). Don't be a sitting duck for your adversary—take cover and encouragement through His vehicle upon the earth, His Church.

Enjoy His presence as you receive direction that comes through times of assembly. Welcome the emotional, physical, and spiritual healing that come through the Body of Christ. You'll find life's answers now for your family problems, your business needs, and what personally concerns you.

Your strength will be multiplied as you meet and serve together. The Church is life itself in the presence of God. He has ordained this provision until we see Him face to face!

A Model of Heaven

Because God intends the Church to be a true model of Heaven's society, it is also meant to be a blessing. That means a local church should be a model of Heaven's love, care, concern, and revelation.

Unfortunately, many churches more accurately model hell. If that is the case for your church, you're better off finding another one!

However, even the best model doesn't compare with the real thing. A model is only an incomplete replica of the real, much like a cardboard mock-up of a new building. Although it can't hold a candle to the final version, it does allow you to see what the finished product should be and to wait expectantly for it.

As we model Heaven through the Church, we can give others a minute glimpse of the real thing. One authentic glimpse of the reality of Heaven could provoke a person to salvation—or at least to investigating what we now know to be a most eternal reward!

Consider how the local church can model these realities of Heaven:

1. *In Heaven, there is the glorious presence of God and an ever-expanding knowledge of who He is and what He has created.*

   In the Church, there is the glorious presence of God and an ever-expanding knowledge of who He is and what He has created. Jesus said, "For where two or three are gathered together in My name, there am I in the midst of them" (Mt. 18:20). God intends for anyone coming in the door to sense the presence and the love of God, and to continue to grow in revelation.

2. *In Heaven, there is loving worship to the Lord. There is singing, praise, and music.*

In the Church, there is loving worship to the Lord. Likewise, there is singing, praise, and music.

3. *In Heaven, there is service to the Lord.* His own serve Him forever out of a heart of gratitude for His goodness.

   In the Church, there is service to the Lord. Believers serve Him as they recognize His great Gift of salvation and understand that their lives are no longer their own.

4. *In Heaven, there is government and structure.* There is no chaos. God rules from His throne. Around Him are 24 elders. There are servers or deacons abounding. There is delegated authority in Heaven.

   In the Church, there is structure as outlined in the Bible. There are apostles, prophets, evangelists, pastors, teachers, elders, and deacons. There is also delegated authority.

5. *In Heaven, there are meaningful eternal relationships.* There are relationships with God first and then with others—and the wonderful reunion and restoration with all who call on His name.

   In the Church, there are meaningful eternal relationships. There are relationships with God first and then with others—and the care, comfort, and transparency to grow together and strengthen one another. This will be a privilege of believers for all eternity.

6. *In Heaven, there is the ministry of angels.* In Heaven, the angels serve God.

In the Church, there is the ministry of angels. On earth, angels are sent to minister to the believer and to serve man (see Heb. 1:14, "ministering spirits").

7. *In Heaven, God's Word is declared. It is law.*

   In the Church, God's Word is declared. It is law!

8. *In Heaven, we live Christ's way. There is acceptance of every person for who he is. We live the law of love.*

   In the Church, we are to live Christ's way. There is to be acceptance of every person regardless of race, culture, or color. We are to model Heaven and live the law of love now.

9. *In Heaven, your destiny is fulfilled.* You achieve the totality for which you were created. Although Heaven is ultimately the place of *God's* fulfillment and destiny, yours comes too as you become one with the Father.

   In the Church, your destiny is started. The "new birth" begins your eternal destiny. Doors of understanding and opportunity begin to open—a process that will continue throughout time.

10. *In Heaven, you find the fullness of a meeting place of God and His people.*

    In the Church, you find the best that Earth can offer as a meeting place for God and His people.

Truly, we are on a pilgrimage to a better country. We have a better and more enduring substance than what we have now. Heaven is our ultimate home.

God has given us His wonderful Church as a model of how Heaven will be. We can share it tangibly with the world. Properly regarded, the Church changes our lives and destinies forever—and helps us meet with God now!

Yet we still have before us *the* city whose builder and maker is God! Of that place, it can be said:

> *...Eye hath not seen, nor ear heard, neither have entered into the heart of man, the things which God hath prepared for them that love Him.*
>
> 1 Corinthians 2:9

It took God six days to make the atmosphere and stars; the planets, lakes, streams, and oceans; all the animals, birds, and man. Yet God has spent 2,000 years working on His city, and He's not finished yet!

Let's see what else God has to say about so real a *place....*

Chapter 2

Heaven Is a Real Place

When God gives us information about something, it's usually because He thinks we need it. He must have felt that way about Heaven.

The word *Heaven* is used at least 568 times in the Bible. Because of our misconceptions and our preconceived notions about Heaven, we usually don't see these Scriptures on Heaven for what they are. We need to take the blinders off our faith and find out what God is really saying!

The Hebrew word for "Heaven" in the Old Testament is *shamayim*. *Shamayim* appears 420 times in the Scriptures.

The New Testament Greek word for "Heaven" is *ouranos*, and *ouranos* is used 148 times.

Both *shamayim* and *ouranos* mean the very same thing: "lofty," or "high"; "above," or "the sky." They are used to refer to high places or elevations.

Yet in order to truly understand what the Bible says about Heaven, or more accurately, "God's Heaven," we must first understand that there are *three* of them. That's right; there are three heavens, and *shamayim* and *ouranos* are used for all three. The Hebrew and the Greek make no distinction. Thus it is vital that we understand the context in which each is used, and to accurately identify to which heaven a verse refers.

This in itself will clarify much of the confusion.

Here are a few verses to help us see the difference:

It is not expedient for me doubtless to glory. I will come to visions and revelations of the Lord.

I knew a man in Christ above fourteen years ago, (whether in the body, I cannot tell; or whether out of the body, I cannot tell: God knoweth;) ***such an one caught up to the third heaven.***

And I knew such a man, (whether in the body, or out of the body, I cannot tell: God knoweth;)

How that he was caught up ***into paradise****, and heard unspeakable words, which it is not lawful for a man to utter.*

Of such an one will I glory: yet of myself I will not glory, but in mine infirmities.

For though I would desire to glory, I shall not be a fool; for I will say the truth: but now I forbear, lest any man should think of me above that which he seeth me to be, or that he heareth of me.

2 Corinthians 12:1-6

The apostle Paul is telling us in this passage about his trip to Heaven. (It's most likely a revelation he gained after being nearly stoned to death at Lystra.)

Notice that Paul mentions he was "caught up to the third heaven," and that he says it was "paradise."

"Paradise" in the Greek is *paradeisos*, which means "the beautiful park of God." Jesus used the exact same word in Revelation 2:7b where He proclaimed, "To him that overcometh will I give to eat of the tree of life, which is in the midst of the paradise of God."

Paradeisos is the *third heaven*, or the Heaven where God dwells. God's Heaven is different from the other two.

The other two heavens are the *atmospheric* and the *astrological* heavens. The atmospheric heaven is made of the clouds, wind, and ozone layer. Simply put, it is the sky above us. It is often referred to in the Scriptures as the "firmament," and merely means the atmosphere or sky.

Above the atmospheric heavens are the astrological heavens. In this heaven, we find the sun, moon, stars, planets, comets, and the Milky Way—in other words, "space." Many times the Word of God refers to this heaven, and not the third heaven, or God's Heaven.

God's Heaven, or the third heaven, is found above the astrological heaven. It is the *paradeisos*, or the "beautiful park of God," and all the wonder that pertains to it.

The apostle Paul was caught up to God's Heaven. The Psalms tell us that God's throne is in this Heaven (see Ps. 11:4). From this majestic place, God rules the universe.

Which Heaven?

There are several examples we can cite for these contexts. Genesis speaks about God creating "the heaven and the earth" (Gen. 1:1). This verse refers not to God's Heaven, but rather to the atmospheric heaven or sky.

We can figure this out because God's Heaven and the astrological heaven (planets, etc.) had already been around for millions of years at the time God made our earth's atmosphere (see Job 38:4-7). One proof is that Lucifer had been thrown out of God's Heaven long before this time (see Lk. 10:18), so the only heaven left to create was the one directly above the earth.

Another example is found in Revelation where John said, "And I saw a new heaven and a new earth: for the first heaven and the first earth were passed away…" (Rev. 21:1).

Again this passage could not be referring to God's Heaven. God had made the place of His throne perfect and eternal, and it would not make any sense for Him to destroy His Heaven and remake it later.

So instead this verse must refer to the atmospheric heaven. We understand through the Book of Revelation that there is coming a day when God will destroy the heaven above us and remake it.

We know for a fact that our atmospheric heaven has been polluted. The ozone layer is currently being destroyed. We've dumped millions of tons of garbage into our skies, and if it is to ever be perfect again, it must be burned up and made new. God promises that He will do just that!

So we now see that God's Heaven is a place separate and distinct from what we commonly think of as the heavens. It's a real place above the atmospheric and astrological heavens that we can readily see.

Could this far-off Heaven be a planet somewhere? The weight of biblical evidence seems to indicate so.

More Than Earth

To conceive of God's Heaven as a planet may throw you at first, yet the intricacy of its scriptural definition certainly leads us to this conclusion.

Make no mistake: We are not talking about something as basic as the planet Earth as we know it. God's Heaven and surroundings would be exceedingly superior. His habitation would be a far more glorious abode, totally free from any pollutants caused by man's sin. Yet the numerous descriptive verses we are given about this Heaven seem to point to a created place that is not too different from earth. In fact, it appears Heaven could be quite like the earth appeared before the fall of man.

That makes sense when you consider how consistent God is in His creations. If God made man in His own image and likeness (and He did), it follows that He would place man in surroundings similar to His own.

We know God made the earth to "fit" man, and so it wonderfully does. We also know that God Himself was quite comfortable here! God enjoyed walking with Adam in the Garden of Eden (see Gen. 3). (In fact, the name "Garden of Eden" also means the "beautiful park of God.")

In another parallel, we know that Enoch went to Heaven without having ever died. This is an Old Testament type of a New Testament "rapture." The Scriptures tell us, "And Enoch walked with God: and he was not; for God took him"

(Gen. 5:24). Evidently, then, man can function in Heaven—for Enoch is still alive!

Elijah also was caught up into Heaven without ever having died (see 2 Kings 2). According to the references in the Word of God, that means Enoch has been in Heaven more than 5,150 years and Elijah more than 3,510. To the best of our knowledge, they are still alive, enjoying life on planet Heaven. Something must be similar, though superior!

A further weight of evidence is that the Second Adam, Jesus, was sent to earth to live among men. This also denotes a compatibility. Heaven's occupant became earth's occupant—and God's Son did well on earth. The Bible makes it clear that the inverse can also happen. Redeemed man, who receives Jesus as Lord, can occupy earth now and Heaven later.

There's an important point to make, however. We need to understand that it is not our human needs or state that ban us from being able to live in Heaven; rather, sin does. Obviously man could live there if there was no sin. Adam would not have had any problem living in Heaven before the fall. Thank God He made a way to take care of our sin that we might inherit the right to eternal life in His Heaven!

A final evidence appears in the Book of Revelation:

And I saw a new heaven and a new earth: for the first heaven and the first earth were passed away; and there was no more sea.

And I John saw the ***holy city, new Jerusalem, coming down from God out of heaven****, prepared as a bride adorned for her husband.*

And I heard a great voice out of heaven saying, Behold, the tabernacle of God is with men, and He will dwell with them, and they shall be His people, and God Himself shall be with them, and be their God.

Revelation 21:1-3

And he carried me away in the spirit to a great and high mountain, and shewed me that ***great city, the holy Jerusalem, descending out of heaven from God.***

Revelation 21:10

We are told that there is a day coming when God's own holy city will descend out of Heaven to the earth. In order for this city to fit in its place on the "new" earth, there must be some kind of planetary similarity! (In a later chapter, we'll look at the word *new*, which means "recreated," as opposed to an entirely separate creation.)

A City of Size

When you read the description of the New Jerusalem in Revelation chapters 21 and 22, you find that the city of New Jerusalem is 1500 miles wide, 1500 miles long, and 1500 miles high. That's a pretty big city! That means planet Heaven must be at least as large as earth. Quite possibly it is much larger.

When you consider that the United States is now preparing a five-acre space station for Mars, would anything be too difficult for our God to prepare, or for that matter, relocate?

We may not know all the details, but there is one thing of which we can be sure: The New Jerusalem is a tangible city. It can be seen and touched. It will come down to a tangible earth—a remade earth, but earth. All that simply means "Heaven is real." Our city is now being prepared!

Tangible Things

What kinds of things can we expect in Heaven?

We're seeing that the planet Heaven is a very real place just like planet Earth is a very real place. The apostle Paul gives us a great confirmation when he says, "The invisible things of God in Heaven are like the visible things of earth" (Rom. 1:20, Dake's translation). Simply put, the things in Heaven are like many things we see on earth!

Again, we see God's continuity. Just as Church life models the Kingdom of God on earth, so earth models life on the planet Heaven. Numerous similarities are written in the Word of God. Just as on earth, Heaven has *trees*. We'll have a chance to eat of the "tree of life, which is in the midst of the paradise of God" (Rev. 2:7).

Likewise, there are *rivers* in Heaven (see Rev. 22:1). There is *gold* and all manner of *precious stones* (see Rev. 21:12-21). There are *mountains* (see Rev. 21:10) and *animals*. (At least, there are *horses*, which suggests some type of animal life [see Rev. 19:11].) If there are animals, there must be *grass*!

There are also *clouds* in Heaven (see Rev. 10:1). There are *fountains*; that is, there are waterfalls or lively spouts of water (see Rev. 7:17). Also, there are *streets* (see Rev. 21:21), *palm leaves*, which means there must also be palm trees (see Rev. 7:9), *fruits* (see Rev. 22:2), and *musical instruments* (see Rev. 5:8).

There is also mention of *food, furniture, clothing, books, crowns, rainbows, thunder and lightning, song, lamps, door-posts, walls, gates*, and *banquets*.

In short, Heaven is very real!

We must forever discard the image of Heaven as some imaginary ghost town covered in mist with nondescript creatures floating about. We must surrender our notion that Heaven is a sort of nothingness. Heaven can be seen and felt. It is inhabited in much the same way as earth. Just because we cannot see it now does not mean it is not real. We must take God at His Word!

An Actual Place

The Word of God is very clear. In the Book of Isaiah, God says:

> *For thus saith the high and lofty One that inhabiteth eternity, whose name is Holy; I dwell in the high and holy* ***place****....*
>
> Isaiah 57:15

"Place" in the Greek is *topos*, meaning a "spot, location, or home." In this case, we've seen that God's Heaven and the New Jerusalem are indeed a spot, location, or home. We've seen that our treasure there is of a "better and more enduring substance." In short, we're headed for a real place of better and more enduring substance!

Jesus Himself tells us so as He encourages His disciples in the Book of John. His disciples are downcast at the prospect of His impending crucifixion and death, for they believe they shall not see Him again.

Let not your heart be troubled: ye believe in God, believe also in Me.

In My Father's house are many mansions: if it were not so, I would have told you. I go to prepare a ***place*** *for you.*

John 14:1-2

He is preparing a real place!

We must change our thinking and become more comfortable with the fact that the Bible presents Heaven as more real than the earth. According to the Word of God, Heaven is the reality, and our life on earth is the shadow:

Now of the things which we have spoken this is the sum: We have such an high priest, who is set on the right hand of the throne of the Majesty in the heavens;

A minister of the sanctuary, and of the true tabernacle, which the Lord pitched, and not man.

For every high priest is ordained to offer gifts and sacrifices: wherefore it is of necessity that this man have somewhat also to offer.

For if He were on earth, He should not be a priest, seeing that there are priests that offer gifts according to the law:

Who serve unto the ***example and shadow of heavenly things****, as Moses was admonished of God when he was about to make the tabernacle: for, See, saith He, that thou make all things according to the pattern shewed to thee in the mount.*

Hebrews 8:1-5

Jesus is telling us that He is in Heaven as our true Priest and example of what is real. The last verse speaks of a pattern; the Greek word *tupos* there means "model" or "statue." We are told that our earthly rituals and ministers merely "serve unto the example and shadow of heavenly things." Simply put, earthly things are a shadow of what is real in Heaven!

The New International Version says, "They [the earthly priests] serve at a sanctuary that is a copy and shadow of what is in heaven" (Heb. 8:5a). That means the Old Testament temple is only a copy of what is in Heaven.

The Amplified Bible, which parallels the original Greek, states that earthly priests offer "service [merely] as a pattern and as a foreshadowing of [what has *its true existence and reality in*] *the heavenly sanctuary*" (Heb. 8:5a).

That shows we are not headed for some unreal, nonexistent place. As Christians, we are headed for Heaven, the place of true reality!

True Realities

Understanding that we are surrounded by mere models or patterns that have their true existence and reality in Heaven gives us insight and cause for hope now.

Much of what we experience on earth seems so unreal, and often impossible to understand. But we are headed for the place of full reality and total understanding. In Heaven, there are no types, shadows, or figurative things:

> *For Christ is not entered into the holy places made with hands, which are the* ***figures of the true****; but into*

heaven itself, now to appear in the presence of God for us.

Hebrews 9:24

The word for "figure" in this verse is the Greek word *antitupon*, meaning a "form" or "model." The Hebrews commonly used this word to mean a sculpture or statue of someone. Although a sculpture may be a good likeness, it is not the real thing. Likewise, the earthly temple of Moses was only a model of the true one where the Lord Himself abides.

The real thing is in Heaven! It is not Heaven that is figurative; it is earth.

The sad truth of the matter is that most of us believe the exact opposite. The devil has been quite successful in making us picture reality backwards. We're usually convinced that the earth we see is all there is and that Heaven is figurative...when the Word of God says just the opposite is true!

When you think about it on God's terms, why shouldn't the eternal be more real than the temporal? We must stop relying on our senses to validate our perceptions. Just as our spiritual identity is more real and eternal than our flesh, so is our unseen eternal home more real than our earthly dwelling.

The Final Pieces

It is true that we will not know the full reality of Heaven until we get there. At best, we will see shadows or glimpses of it. But we can rest assured: The real thing is coming! The third heaven is just as real as the atmospheric heaven we see now. When we behold the real thing, our earthly existence will fade from memory like the shadowed model it was always intended to be.

Yet such reality is not assured for those who do not know Jesus as their High Priest and Lord. Without access to His truth, no man can ever know true reality or his own eternal destiny. Such a person can only live in the "shadows" of life until he dies, when he will enter an eternity of nonfulfillment. The puzzle pieces of his life will remain forever scattered.

Next to being cast away from the presence of God Himself, that has to be the most terrible reality of hell. Thank God, we are called to live forever with our great God in a real place called Heaven.

Chapter 3

Locating Heaven

One purpose of faith is to help us become more comfortable with the reality of what we cannot see or understand. Still, when the Scriptures give us a more specific understanding of a truth, it makes sense to search it out. Then we can more fully give an account for the hope that is within us.

Because the weight of biblical evidence indicates that Heaven is most likely a planet, we need to search out references that help us determine its location.

Here's where our study becomes more difficult. There's a very real challenge whenever natural man tries to describe the things of God. A best, we only see through a "glass, darkly" (1 Cor. 13:12).

Nevertheless, the Word of God has some important things to say that help us in our quest. The first concerns the approximate direction of Heaven.

Quite simply, Heaven is "up," or "out," from earth. That's important to state. Though it may seem obvious, you'd be surprised at how many people have it confused. The devil has succeeded for thousands of years in convincing millions upon millions of people that "this is it." They have bought the lie that this earth is the only Heaven they'll ever get, and that when they die, their souls sleep forever.

Satan's next ploy was the false "hope" of reincarnation. Other millions have bought the lie that after this life, they'll come back to earth in another life form. The bottom line of this story also makes earth the only "Heaven."

The Christian may think both reincarnation and "heaven on earth" are foolish beliefs, but unfortunately multiplied millions of people have and do believe it the world over. The Buddhists and the Hindus believe it, and live like they do. Hindus literally starve to death rather than kill a cow and eat it because they fear it might be someone they knew!

The United States is no exception. Prominent people believe in reincarnation, and mislead thousands with their testimonies. All over the globe, untold multitudes of people are being robbed not only of their hope in Heaven, but also of the joy of their salvation!

The reincarnation myth began in ancient Egypt more than 4,000 years ago. Egyptian philosophers watched a pregnant scarab beetle roll up in the mud and die. After it died, several little beetles were born and came crawling out of the mud. These wise philosophers then assumed that many lives were spawned out of death. When a person dies, they believed that person would get another opportunity to come back and start again!

According to God's law, this simply isn't so. The Word of God tells us that it is appointed to man once to die, and after that, judgment (see Heb. 9:27). Then it's to Heaven or hell, not back to earth for another chance as a beetle, a cow—or as Henry the Eighth.

Convincing Proofs

Thank God the earth is not Heaven; we await a far superior place—and it is "up"! The apostle Paul was clear about this from his own heavenly visit:

> *It is not expedient for me doubtless to glory. I will come to visions and revelations of the Lord.*
>
> *I knew a man in Christ above fourteen years ago, (whether in the body, I cannot tell; or whether out of the body, I cannot tell: God knoweth;) such an one* ***caught up to the third heaven.***
>
> *And I knew such a man, (whether in the body, or out of the body, I cannot tell: God knoweth;)*
>
> *How that he was caught up into paradise, and heard unspeakable words, which it is not lawful for a man to utter.*
>
> *Of such an one will I glory: yet of myself I will not glory, but in mine infirmities.*
>
> *For though I would desire to glory, I shall not be a fool; for I will say the truth: but now I forbear, lest any man should think of me above that which he seeth me to be, or that he heareth of me.*
>
> 2 Corinthians 12:1-6

As we've seen, there are three heavens: the atmospheric, the astrological, and God's Heaven. In these verses, Paul makes it clear he was above the first two heavens and into the third.

That means God's Heaven is somewhere above the astrological heavens, above the sun, moon, and stars—no doubt billions of light years away. But it's *up*!

There are 38 more Scripture passages that specifically say Heaven is "up," along with a host of others that also imply it. Here are a few of them:

> *Know therefore this day, and consider it in thine heart, that the Lord He is God in heaven* ***above****, and upon the earth beneath: there is none else.*
>
> Deuteronomy 4:39
>
> *Look* ***down*** *from Thy holy habitation, from heaven, and bless Thy people....*
>
> Deuteronomy 26:15
>
> *...He is God in heaven* ***above****, and in earth beneath.*
>
> Joshua 2:11
>
> *God looked* ***down*** *from heaven upon the children of men....*
>
> Psalm 53:2
>
> *Look* ***down*** *from heaven, and behold from the habitation of Thy holiness and of Thy glory.*
>
> Isaiah 63:15a
>
> *...the angel of the Lord* ***descended from heaven****, and came and rolled back the stone from the door, and sat upon it.*
>
> Matthew 28:2

*So then after the Lord had spoken unto them, He was received **up into heaven**, and sat on the right hand of God.*

Mark 16:19

*...He was parted from them, and carried **up** into heaven.*

Luke 24:51

*For the bread of God is He which cometh **down** from heaven, and giveth life unto the world.*

John 6:33

*For I came **down** from heaven, not to do Mine own will, but the will of Him that sent Me.*

John 6:38

Here is perhaps the most familiar passage about a day soon approaching:

*For the Lord Himself shall **descend** from heaven with a shout, with the voice of the archangel, and with the trump of God: and the dead in Christ shall rise first:*

Then we which are alive and remain shall be caught up together with them in the clouds to meet the Lord in the air: and so shall we ever be with the Lord.

1 Thessalonians 4:16-17

Scriptural Clues

Other than "up," are there any more specific directions about Heaven's location? There are several verses that seem to indicate that the planet Heaven is in the *northernmost* part of our universe, beyond the astrological heaven.

An in-depth look at Psalm 75 gives us one such example:

Unto Thee, O God, do we give thanks, unto Thee do we give thanks: for that Thy name is near Thy wondrous works declare.

When I shall receive the congregation I will judge uprightly.

The earth and all the inhabitants thereof are dissolved: I bear up the pillars of it. Selah.

I said unto the fools, Deal not foolishly: and to the wicked, Lift not up the horn:

Lift not up your horn on high: speak not with a stiff neck.

For promotion cometh neither from the east, nor from the west, nor from the south.

But God is the judge: He putteth down one, and setteth up another.

Psalm 75:1-7

This is a psalm of Asaph regarding the relationship of God to man and the earth. It's a song that prophesies Christ's coming rule and reign during the Millennium.

The second to the last verse quoted above speaks about promotion, and this is where a vital point is made. This verse states that promotion does not come from the east, west, or south; rather, it comes from God.

Notice that there is a direction missing. North is not stated. This infers that God, who causes promotion, dwells in that northernmost direction. This common literary technique makes a point by drawing attention to the obvious omission. There is an east, west, and south, but God Himself replaces the north. His upright judgment comes from that direction.

There are plenty of other references regarding the importance of the north. Another is found in Isaiah; it concerns the fall of the devil out of Heaven:

> *How art thou fallen from heaven, O Lucifer, son of the morning! how art thou cut down to the ground, which didst weaken the nations!*
>
> *For thou hast said in thine heart, I will ascend into heaven, I will exalt my throne above the stars of God: I will sit also upon the mount of the congregation, in the sides of the* ***north***.
>
> Isaiah 14:12-13

In this account, we see that lucifer himself has said that he will take God's place and rule upon the mount of the congregation in the *sides* of the *north*. The Hebrew word for "sides" is *yerekah*, meaning "rear, rear flank, rear quarter, or hind quarter."

Simply put, lucifer literally attempted a spiritual *coup d'etat* on the planet Heaven, and he set his sights on the *rear quarter of the north* of the universe.

Rotherham's translation of the Hebrew in verse 13 states, "Thou didst say in thy heart, the heavens will I ascend; above the stars of God will I lift my throne, that I may sit *in the recesses of the North—in place of God*."

J.B. Phillips' translation says, "I will set up my throne on high that I may rule in the far places of the North."

Kenneth Taylor's paraphrased version exclaims, "For you said to yourself, 'I will ascend to heaven and rule the angels. I will take the highest throne. I will preside on the Mount of Assembly far away in the north.' "

Taken together, these verses indicate that the best calculation for Heaven's location is above the astrological heavens in the northernmost part of the universe. Heaven is quite possibly just beyond the northernmost boundaries of our universe.

A final verse from Job pulls much of these clues together and provides an interesting parallel that scientists have recently discovered. Perhaps Heaven is located beyond the huge black hole found to the north of our universe.

> *He stretcheth out the north over the empty place, and hangeth the earth upon nothing.*
>
> Job 26:7

A massive "black hole" has long been suspected to exist in our universe, but only recently confirmed and reported by scientists. Scientists found that you can arc light into this hole, but light will not come out. The hole itself is located in a galaxy 21 million light years from Earth, and is estimated to be a mass equal to 40 million of our suns. An interesting discovery![1]

Far From Hell

No matter what exact location God's Heaven holds in the northernmost parts, there is a very clear scriptural promise about it. Heaven is the farthest point in the universe from the devil's home in hell!

When God brought an end to the devil's *coup d'etat*, He made sure lucifer would have the leadership he so desired in "the sides of the north"—in *hell*!

> *How art thou fallen from heaven, O Lucifer, son of the morning! how art thou cut down to the ground, which didst weaken the nations!*
>
> *For thou hast said in thine heart, I will ascend into heaven, I will exalt my throne above the stars of God: I will sit also upon the mount of the congregation, in the sides of the* ***north****:*
>
> *I will ascend above the heights of the clouds; I will be like the most High.*
>
> ***Yet thou shalt be brought down to hell, to the sides of the pit.***
>
> *They that see thee shall narrowly look upon thee, and consider thee, saying, Is this the man that made the earth to tremble, that did shake kingdoms;*
>
> *That made the world as a wilderness, and destroyed the cities thereof; that opened not the house of his prisoners?*
>
> Isaiah 14:12-17

The Hebrew word for "sides" in verse 15 is *yerekah*, the same as in verse 13. Satan's grand scheme to ascend to the highest parts of the north, to the rear quarter of Heaven, was replaced by an assignment to the lowest parts of hell. In fact, the literal Hebrew describes the location as the "rear end of hell"!

That means if you measure the distance from the highest parts of the north (God's habitation) to the lowest parts of the pit of hell, you'll discover that lucifer will be the farthest thing from God.

As a resident of Heaven, that also means the devil will be the farthest thing from you! There will be no grief for you in Heaven; no pain or sickness; no poverty or death. These things will be far from you, for their author has been cast down. He has indeed "fallen from heaven like lightning" (see Lk. 10:18).

Remember that as you await your eternal home, God's Heaven, in the north of the universe. Think on that place of His eternal presence, far from the enemy of your soul.

Surely that is paradise!

Endnote

1. Hugh Ross, videotape lecture "Reasons to Believe" (P.O. Box 5978, Pasadena, CA 91117); also Stephen W. Hawking, *A Brief History of Time* (Toronto: Bantam Books, 1988), 81-82.

Chapter 4

Your Glorified Body

Just as we have seen that Heaven is a real place, we'll see that there are real beings in Heaven that lead fulfilling lives. In fact, they are not all that unlike you and me!

When you consider that God has used the Church on earth to model Heaven's society, and the planet Earth to model the place called Heaven, it follows that He would also use the people of earth to foreshadow eternal beings!

Forget a bunch of figurative ghosts on a mist-like cloud. Remember that the things of Heaven are far more real and eternal than the "figurative" things of earth. It is actually the things of earth that are "shadows" of what has "true existence and reality" in Heaven (see Heb. 8:5).

This means spirit beings would have actual bodies. Just because you can't see them doesn't mean they don't exist. On the other hand, though they may be similar to us in appearance, they would function quite differently. The temporary bodies we have here on earth would be far more limiting than the wonders of our eternal form.

Limited Dimensions

Our earthly bodies are bound to this earth. We live temporarily within the three dimensions we commonly know: height, length, and width.

Our spiritual bodies would not be bound by those limitations. Instead, we shall be able to enjoy life with God in the fullness of every dimension in which He Himself exists.

"According to the science of particle physics, we know that at least 11 dimensions exist, though scientists cannot tell us how to access them."[1] Still, Jesus, in His glorified body, was able to pass through walls (see Jn. 20:19). Scientists tell us that this is conceptually possible in the sixth dimension. Since we are to become like Him (see Phil. 3:21), we too shall know the liberty of added dimensions. In God's presence, there may be far more than the 11 we know!

A Model of a Glorified Body

The apostle Paul gave us some incredible insight into how our spiritual or glorified bodies would appear:

> *It is not expedient for me doubtless to glory. I will come to visions and revelations of the Lord.*
>
> *I knew a man in Christ above fourteen years ago,* ***(whether in the body, I cannot tell; or whether out of the body, I cannot tell: God knoweth;) such an one caught up to the third heaven.***
>
> *And I knew such a man, (whether in the body, or out of the body, I cannot tell: God knoweth;)*

How that he was caught up into paradise, and heard unspeakable words, which it is not lawful for a man to utter.

2 Corinthians 12:1-4

This event happened to Paul personally, most likely in Lystra where he had been stoned to death for his stand for Christ. As the disciples gathered around his body and prayed, Paul was raised from the dead. Apparently during the short time he was dead, Paul had been caught up to Heaven.

Notice that there was no question in Paul's mind about where he had gone. He knew for certain that he had been "caught up to the third heaven," or the paradise of God.

However, Paul could not tell whether he was in his body or out of it at the time! Twice he tells us that he did not know the difference. This must mean that our glorified bodies are very similar in appearance, since he could not discern between them!

While Paul was in Heaven, he must have had contact with other spiritual beings. He must have seen how they looked. No doubt God had a direct purpose planned for this encounter, just as He did for the apostle John and others who recorded similar experiences.

Paul's inability to tell whether he was in his body or in the spirit at the time, gives us many answers to our questions about how we shall appear.

Through additional Scriptures, we shall see that while we may be similar, our heavenly or spiritual bodies shall be far superior. We shall also see that imperfections will be removed.

You'll find that you will probably look better in Heaven than you do now, but you will be recognizably you.

Fashioned Like Him

No doubt our most important example of our glorified appearance is provided by Jesus Himself. Philippians says that our dying bodies will be changed "into glorious bodies like His own" (Phil. 3:21; Kenneth Taylor's translation).

Therefore, what we can determine about the body of Jesus after His own resurrection can give us more insight about what we will be like. We know from that verse in Philippians tha we will be changed to be like Him when we die or are raptured.

The Gospel of John gives us specifics about how Jesus appeared after His resurrection:

But Mary stood without at the sepulchre weeping: and as she wept, she stooped down, and looked into the sepulchre,

And seeth two angels in white sitting, the one at the head, and the other at the feet, where the body of Jesus had lain.

And they say unto her, Woman, why weepest thou? She saith unto them, Because they have taken away my Lord, and I know not where they have laid Him.

And when she had thus said, she turned herself back, and saw Jesus standing, and knew not that it was Jesus.

Jesus saith unto her, Woman, why weepest thou? whom seekest thou? She, supposing Him to be the gardener, saith unto Him, Sir, if Thou have borne Him hence, tell me where Thou hast laid Him, and I will take Him away.

Jesus saith unto her, Mary. She turned herself, and saith unto Him, Rabboni; which is to say, Master.

Jesus saith unto her, Touch Me not; for I am not yet ascended to My Father: but go to My brethren, and say unto them, I ascend unto My Father, and your Father; and to My God, and your God.

John 20:11-17

In this passage, Mary Magdalene is bringing spices to embalm the body of Jesus and finds the tomb empty. We know that Jesus had been resurrected, but Mary is very distraught and weeps profusely. She thinks that the gardeners have moved Him, and she does not know where to find His body.

When she turns around, she sees a man standing there. At first she believes He is a gardener and not Jesus. Indeed it was the Lord, yet there are several reasons why she may not have recognized Him at this point.

Because Mary had been crying and was distraught, her vision may have been clouded. Also, because she expected a gardener, she may not have even looked or considered Him to be anyone else.

Another factor is that it was socially unacceptable at that time for a woman to look at a man's face while speaking. Perhaps Mary did not even glace at the man standing there.

A final but less probable reason to our minds is that Jesus had not yet ascended into Heaven to place His shed blood on

Heaven's altar. In fact, He may have looked a bit different at this point.

However, one conclusion remains clear: Mary was not expecting to see Jesus. Her lapse was momentary, though; when Jesus spoke her name, Mary "turned herself" (verse 16). As she looked at Him, she immediately recognized Jesus. She said, "Rabboni," or "Master." Jesus must have appeared recognizably as Himself.

Evidently Mary must have run toward Him, most likely to embrace Him, for He said, "Don't touch Me yet. I have not yet ascended to Heaven to make atonement with My blood."

Jesus explained this to Mary in detail. He belabored the point that He must yet go up to Heaven to His Father and hers. He then bade her to go and tell the disciples what she had seen and heard.

Many things are clear from this passage. Jesus looked like a man, not a ghost. He had a body she could see, even though He had not yet ascended to the Father and received the fullness of His glorified body.

Also, He could talk. He could hear. He could see. Evidently, His voice was the same because Mary easily recognized it. If we are made to be like Him, then that means we shall also have real, tangible bodies that see, hear, talk, and can be touched.

Other inferences from the passages that follow tell us even more about our heavenly appearance.

According to His words to Mary, Jesus did not want to be touched because He still had to ascend and offer His final sacrifice of blood on the mercy seat and receive His glorified body. The Scriptures indicate that He accomplished this on the same day (which means Heaven can be reached quickly!).

> *Then the same day at evening, being the first day of the week, when the doors were shut where the disciples were assembled for fear of the Jews, came Jesus and stood in the midst, and saith unto them, Peace be unto you.*
>
> *And when He had so said, He shewed unto them His hands and His side. Then were the disciples glad, when they saw the Lord.*
>
> John 20:19-20

When Jesus returned, He came right through the walls and locked doors to appear to His disciples. He transcended our known dimensions, but when He appeared to His own friends, He was very recognizably Himself!

The Gospel of Luke give us further confirmation through another appearance.

The setting is on the road to Emmaus, about four hours after the resurrection. (This Scripture suggests that the round trip to Heaven may take two hours or less!)

Jesus is appearing to two men on the road. After recognizing Him, they hurried back to Jerusalem to tell the disciples about the encounter. As they began to speak, Jesus Himself appeared suddenly in the room, passing through the doors locked by the disciples for fear of the Jews.

> *And as they thus spake, Jesus Himself stood in the midst of them, and saith unto them, Peace be unto you.*

> *But they were terrified and affrighted, and supposed that they had seen a spirit.*
>
> Luke 24:36-37

Knox's translation says, "They thought they were seeing an apparition." Weymouth's translation says, "They were startled and alarmed and thought they were seeing a ghost."

Yet the next passage indicates this:

> *And He said unto them, Why are ye troubled? and why do thoughts arise in your hearts?*
>
> *Behold My hands and My feet, that it is I Myself: handle Me, and see;* ***for a spirit hath not flesh and bones, as ye see Me have.***
>
> *And when He had thus spoken, He shewed them His hands and His feet.*
>
> Luke 24:38-40

In other words, Jesus is saying, "It's really Me. I am not a ghost. See Me. Touch Me. Handle Me." The Greek word in verse 39 for "handle" is *pselaphao*, meaning "touch" or "feel." Jesus invites His disciples to "feel, touch, see that I am real. A ghost doesn't have flesh and bones like I have."

The Greek word for "flesh" is *sarx*, meaning "skin"; and "bones" is *osteon*, meaning "skeletal bones." Jesus is making it very clear that He is not a ghost, for ghost have no bones and skin.

Since the disciples were still amazed, Jesus offered a further proof of the reality of our glorified bodies:

> *And while they yet believed not for joy, and wondered, He said unto them, Have ye here any meat?*

And they gave Him a piece of broiled fish, and of an honeycomb.

And He took it, and did eat before them.

And He said unto them, These are the words which I spake unto you, while I was yet with you, that all things must be fulfilled, which were written in the law of Moses, and in the prophets, and in the psalms, concerning Me.

Then opened He their understanding, that they might understand the scriptures,

And said unto them, Thus it is written, and thus it behoved Christ to suffer, and to rise from the dead the third day.

Luke 24:41-46

In His mercy, Jesus offered an ultimate proof that He was not an apparition or a ghost. He asked for something to eat. Ghosts don't eat!

In short, the Lord went to great lengths to prove He was real. He proved that heavenly bodies are real. We too have the promise of being conformed to His very image!

That means we too shall be gloriously free of the limitations of our earthly flesh. In fact, that is God's intention:

For our **conversation** *is in heaven; from whence also we look for the Saviour, the Lord Jesus Christ:*

Who shall change our vile body, that it may be fashioned like unto His glorious body, according to the working whereby He is able even to subdue all things unto Himself.

Philippians 3:20-21

You see, our true "citizenship" is in Heaven! This word appears as "conversation" in the verse above. However, in Greek, "conversation" is *politeuma*, meaning a "community, township, or citizenship." (Our word *politician* comes from it, for a politician represents the citizens.)

Here the apostle Paul is telling us that God's highest intent is for us, His children, to be the "townspeople of Heaven." Our true citizenship is there! We will look and behave like the true citizens of Heaven in all their glorious liberty!

Moffatt's translation says, "We are a colony of heaven." Weymouth's translation says, "We are free citizens of heaven." Goodspeed's translation of the Greek to English says, "The commonwealth to which we belong is heaven."

That means our true destiny is to be "looking to Heaven for the coming of our Saviour, the Lord Jesus Christ, who will change us to be like His glorious body to live in Heaven as citizens forever!"

Transfigured

Thus in order to be a citizen of Heaven, our physical bodies must be changed (see 1 Cor. 15:51-55). The Greek word for "change" is called a "picture word." Picture words are a popular technique the Greeks used to visually and dramatically explain a definition.

"Change" is *metaschematizo*, which means to "transfigure," or "a change in condition," but not a total transformation. The picture word is of a garden and the changes you might make in it.

For example, last year you may have planted corn and beans in your garden, but this year you planted corn, beans, and squash. You changed the scheme, or *metaschematizo*, but the structure is still a garden.

When people see your garden, they don't ask you why you got rid of your garden. They still recognize it as a garden, even though it has changed somewhat. This is how the Word of God describes our bodies being changed.

Notice that the word is not *metamorphoos*, or "transformation," which is "the process of change from one state of being to another." That word in our English derivative is *metamorphosis*, and is found in Romans where it speaks about "renewing our natural mind" (see Rom. 12:2).

A word picture of *metamorphoos* would be a whole different concept. *Metamorphoos* means that you would plow up the garden and make it into a softball field. It is that type of transformation.

However, this will not be the case with our natural bodies when they are changed. God will not "plow you up" and make you into something entirely different. Rather, He will *metaschematizo* you—change your scheme a bit. He adds something to the garden; He adds to your dimensions.

You will still be you, only gloriously better. He shall "change our vile body, that it may be fashioned like unto His glorious body" (Phil. 3:21a). The Greek word for "fashion" is *summorphos*, meaning to "shape or make similar."

The New English Bible puts it this way, "To give our bodies the form like that of his own resplendent body or form."

Taylor's paraphrased says to "change" our bodies "into glorious bodies like His own."

The Amplified Bible says that Christ will "fashion anew the body of our humiliation to conform to and be like the body of His glory and majesty, by exerting that power which enables Him even to subject everything to Himself."

All this means we shall be like Him! We shall have a real appearance. Our glorified bodies will have skin and bone. We will walk, talk, see, hear, taste, touch, and smell. We will eat and drink.

In Heaven we will see real people, touch them, recognize them, and hear their voices. As citizens of Heaven, we will live with God in His unshadowed and unhindered dimensions forever.

Yet there is even more to Heaven made real!

Endnote

1. Hugh Ross, *The Fingerprint of God* (Orange, CA: Promise Publishing Co., 1989), 180.

Chapter 5

Your Proper Self

What a wonder to discover that we shall look like ourselves in glory. Yet is there more that can be known about how we shall be changed?

An important passage in First Corinthians solves a lot of the mystery:

> *But some man will say, How are the dead raised up? and with what body do they come?*
>
> *Thou fool, that which thou sowest is not quickened, except it die:*
>
> ***And that which thou sowest, thou sowest not that body that shall be, but bare grain, it may chance of wheat, or of some other grain:***
>
> *But God giveth it a body as it hath pleased Him, and* ***to every seed his own body.***
>
> ***All flesh is not the same flesh:*** *but there is one kind of flesh of men, another flesh of beasts, another of fishes, and another of birds.*

There are also celestial bodies, and bodies terrestrial: *but the glory of the celestial is one, and the glory of the terrestrial is another.*

There is one glory of the sun, and another glory of the moon, and another glory of the stars: for one star differeth from another star in glory.

So also is the resurrection of the dead. ***It is sown in corruption; it is raised in incorruption:***

It is sown in dishonour; it is raised in glory: it is sown in weakness; it is raised in power:

It is sown a natural body; it is raised a spiritual body. There is a natural body, and there is a spiritual body.

And so it is written, The first man Adam was made a living soul; the last Adam was made a quickening spirit.

Howbeit that was not first which is spiritual, but that which is natural, and afterward that which is spiritual.

The first man is of the earth, earthy: the second man is the Lord from heaven.

As is the earthy, such are they also that are earthy: and as is the heavenly, such are they also that are heavenly.

And as we have borne the image of the earthy, we shall also bear the image of the heavenly.

Now this I say, brethren, that flesh and blood cannot inherit the kingdom of God; neither doth corruption inherit incorruption.

Behold, I shew you a mystery; We shall not all sleep, but we shall all be changed,

In a moment, in the twinkling of an eye, at the last trump: for the trumpet shall sound, and the dead shall be raised incorruptible, and we shall be changed.

For this corruptible must put on incorruption, and this mortal must put on immortality.

So when this corruptible shall have put on incorruption, and this mortal shall have put on immortality, then shall be brought to pass the saying that is written, Death is swallowed up in victory.

O death, where is thy sting? O grave, where is thy victory?

The sting of death is sin; and the strength of sin is the law.

But thanks be to God, which giveth us the victory through our Lord Jesus Christ.

Therefore, my beloved brethren, be ye stedfast, unmoveable, always abounding in the work of the Lord, forasmuch as ye know that your labour is not in vain in the Lord.

1 Corinthians 15:35-58

Knox's translation of verse 35 says, "What kind of bodies will they be wearing when they appear?"

These questions cover it all: What we will look like; what color we will be; what race, what size, and what nationality? Hidden in verses 36 and 37 is the simple answer: When you plant a kernel of wheat, it dies, and then is resurrected as wheat. It does not come up cabbage, but wheat.

Through biology, we know that there is an inner code written into the wheat that does not change even though the kernel died. It must come up whatever it was.

God Himself established that law of "sowing and reaping." What you sow, you will reap (see Gal. 6:7). This principle will not cease throughout eternity. That means when you die, you will be raised up as you. You will be glorified, and you may operate in added dimensions, but it really is you!

Notice verse 38. This verse compares men and women to seeds. It says every seed gets "*his own body*." Let that truth deal a final blow to any misconceptions that may exist about reincarnation!

When you go to Heaven, God does not change the type of body you will inhabit. There is no arbitrary switching of people or species. God is too structured for such folly. Furthermore, it would not be like Him to alter the integrity and intimacy with which He has created you personally.

Simply put, you will either be resurrected to life everlasting in Heaven, or to life everlasting in hell, as you. You will not get another chance in another body! "...It is appointed unto men once to die, but after this the judgment" (Heb. 9:27).

Idios Self

"If we receive our own body upon resurrecting, will it appear exactly the same?" you ask.

The Greek for "own" body is *idios*, meaning "that which pertains to self-identity"; that which "makes you uniquely you"; or that which is "privately you."

Therefore, when you are raised in glory, what makes you "uniquely you" would remain the same. That includes the color, size, shape, characteristics, features, appearance, and gender you currently are. However, there would be some wonderful and important differences.

Certain physical disorders would not be carried over into your glorified body. If you are crippled now, you would not be crippled in your glorified body. If you are blind now, you would not be blind on that day. If your body is 200 pounds overweight, that would not be the case for your glorified body.

How can we know this? The Word tells us that we will be raised as our *idios*, or proper self. This literally means your "self" in *proper* order—whatever that means for your personally. The inference is that when you enter into God's eternal dimensions, you are changed to become proper in your own (*idios*) dimensions.

Each of us will enjoy our glorified body, our proper self in proper order, resurrected without flaw. Yet it will be you, down to the color of your hair and eyes, which makes you "uniquely you."

Every Kindred Nation

Likewise, you will be resurrected in the beauty that God originally created you, whatever race and color that may be.

When Jesus appeared again to His disciples, He was brownish olive in color. He still appeared as a Jewish man, and He looked like one. As His disciples inspected Him, they looked at His skin. They touched it. They knew it was Him. He looked the same!

There will be all kinds of people in Heaven, just as we have on earth now:

> *And they sung a new song, saying, Thou art worthy to take the book, and to open the seals thereof: for Thou wast slain, and hast redeemed us to God by Thy blood out of every kindred, and tongue, and people, and nation.*
>
> Revelation 5:9

The Greek word for "kindred" is *phule*, meaning "race" or "clan," while the Greek word for "nation" is *ethnos*, meaning "races" or "tribes." That simply means there will be people in Heaven from every nation, every race, every tribe, and every clan.

The same great God who delighted in creating such diversity in the first place will not be robbed of the same delight in Heaven! However, because of His wonderful reign and transforming power, there will be no prejudice in Heaven. There will be no racial distress because all races and peoples will be in proper order with each other as well.

A Proper Age

In Heaven, as we become all that is "properly" or our *idios* selves, can we draw any conclusions as to what age we might appear? Again, the word *idios* helps us.

Although it is difficult to pinpoint exactly what age we will be, the *idios* self suggests that we would be whatever age we are *properly matured*. For most people, that age is about 30 years old, though it may vary a bit from person to person.

There are two primary examples from Scripture that support this idea. We know that when God first created Adam from the dust, he was mature, or about 30 years old. We know that God made him "properly," or who he was ideally meant to be, and said it was "good" (see Gen. 1:26-31). Adam was created perfect and without flaws; he was mature. The Greek word for "perfect" has within its meaning "fully matured."

Another indicator is Jesus Himself. The Lord was between 30 and 33 years old when He died and received His glorified body. According to God's eternal purpose through His Son, these were the years of His proper self maturity.

As we have already seen, our bodies will be changed to be like unto His glorious body (*sumorphos*, or "similar"; see Phil. 3:21). It makes sense that we would also be similar in age to Him. The weight of evidence suggests that we too will be "thirty something."

Consider the story of Marie Fox, a woman whose personal experience lends great support to this concept:

> "As a young child of nine, I lost my parents to an automobile accident. Though it was a difficult situation, God graciously provided me a home with my aunt and others who loved me as I grew to adulthood.
>
> "During my teen years, there was one very special woman named Zella who was my pastor's wife. She

was much like a mom to me, and to this day, she holds a special place in my heart. When I was 18, I had the privilege of living in her home.

"That is when Zella had the dream about Heaven. In her dream, Zella had not died, but she had been raptured. As she walked around Heaven, she saw the magnificent banqueting table prepared along with indescribably beautiful flowers and plush, green grass.

"As she looked around to see whom she might recognize, she was approached by a couple she did not know. They began to speak to her, saying, 'Thank you, oh, thank you,' while hugging her tightly. Zella asked what they were thanking her for. The woman replied, 'Thank you for taking care of Marie for us.'

"As Zella told me the dream, she described what my parents looked like. I couldn't believe the accuracy and detail she gave of my parents whom she had never met! Had Mom and Dad been alive then, they would have been in their mid-forties, yet Zella described them perfectly as a young 'thirty-something,' the very age at which I had last known my parents when they died!"

An Eternal Body

What about the actual substance of our new bodies? What kind of flesh will they be? The Word of God is quite specific!

> *There are also* ***celestial bodies, and bodies terrestrial****: but the glory of the celestial is one, and the glory of the terrestrial is another.*

There is one glory of the sun, and another glory of the moon, and another glory of the stars: for one star differeth from another star in glory.

So also is the resurrection of the dead. It is sown in corruption; it is raised in incorruption:

It is sown in dishonour; it is raised in glory: it is sown in weakness; it is raised in power:

1 Corinthians 15:40-43

God made two kinds of bodies: "celestial" bodies and "terrestrial" bodies. These simply mean "heavenly" or "earthly," in that sequence. The Amplified Bible makes these verses easier to understand:

There are heavenly bodies (sun, moon, and stars) and there are earthly bodies (men, animals, and plants), but the beauty and glory of the heavenly bodies is of one kind, while the beauty and glory of earthly bodies is a different kind.

The sun is glorious in one way, the moon is glorious in another way, and the stars are glorious in their own [distinctive] way; for one star differs from and surpasses another in its beauty and brilliance.

So it is with the resurrection of the dead. [The body] that is sown is perishable and decays, but [the body] that is resurrected is imperishable (immune to decay, immortal).

It is sown in dishonor and humiliation; it is raised in honor and glory. It is sown in infirmity and weakness; it is resurrected in strength and endued with power.

1 Corinthians 15:40-43

What a promise! What a confident expectation we can have for the glory of our eternal bodies!

Now let's look at the verses that immediately follow:

It is sown a natural body; it is raised a spiritual body. There is a natural body, and there is a spiritual body.

And so it is written, The first man Adam was made a living soul; the last Adam was made a quickening spirit.

Howbeit that was not first which is spiritual, but that which is natural; and afterward that which is spiritual.

1 Corinthians 15:44-46

And also from the Amplified:

Is is sown a natural (physical) body; it is raised a supernatural (a spiritual) body. [As surely as] there is a physical body, there is also a spiritual body.

Thus it is written, The first man Adam became a living being (an individual personality); the last Adam (Christ) became a life-giving Spirit [restoring the dead to life].

But it is not the spiritual life which came first, but the physical and then the spiritual.

1 Corinthians 15:44-46

Quite simply, this means we are born physically before we are born spiritually. So our second, or spiritual, birth gives us a distinctly heavenly appearance:

The first man is of the earth, earthy: the second man is the Lord from heaven.

As is the earthy, such are they also that are earthy: and as is the heavenly, such are they also that are heavenly.

And as we have borne the image of the earthy, we shall also ***bear the image of the heavenly****.*

1 Corinthians 15:47-49

And again, in the Amplified:

The first man [was] from out of earth, made of dust (earthly-minded); the second Man [is] the Lord from out of heaven.

Now those who are made of the dust are like him who was first made of the dust (earthly-minded); and as is [the Man] from heaven, so also [are those] who are of heaven (heavenly-minded).

And just as we have borne the image [of the man] of dust, so shall we and so let us also bear the image [of the Man] of heaven.

1 Corinthians 15:47-49

The Father's Likeness

What kind of heavenly appearance will we have?

The Greek word for "image" in verse 49 is *eikon*, meaning "likeness, a statue, to profile," and can also mean "to model." *Eikon* also means to "look like your parents." This particular Greek meaning is best described by a word picture. The word picture is very descriptive, though perhaps vernacular: It means to be "a spitting image of your father"!

This is the most accurate definition of *eikon*, and it models a tremendous heavenly truth. Just as we have modeled the first man, Adam, made from the dust, so we will model the second Adam, Jesus, the Man from Heaven!

The Greek text of this verse actually reads, "We shall and so let us bear His profile." Simply put, "Let us become the spitting image of Jesus!"

Knox's translation says, "It remains for us who once bore the stamp of earth to now bear the stamp of heaven."

What a privilege—and promise—to bear His image forever! During our time here on earth, we have perpetuated the image of the first Adam. We look like him. Yet our forthcoming spiritual body and likeness shall forever perpetuate the image of the second Adam, Jesus!

Just as Jesus said, "If you've seen Me, you've seen the Father" (see Jn. 14:9), each of us will be able to say the same thing. As His own proud child, you will say, "I am the spitting image of my Father. I look like Him. I bear His image."

In addition to God's profile, we shall also bear His glory when we are raised up (see 1 Cor. 15:43). The entire universe and every being in it will know who we are. It will be written on our countenance that we are sons and daughters of God. This is a privilege to which even the most beautiful angel can never lay claim!

Unfathomable Love

This truth of being called to bear the image of our heavenly Father reveals an even more transcendent wonder: the Father's heart of endless love.

Father God so wanted sons and daughters with whom to share Himself that He created the whole universe to do it. It was not just a matter of shaping clay and breathing into it to create man (see Gen. 2:7). It took far more for Him to create a climate for us to share His life and love.

Recent scientific research is proving that the entire universe plays a part in sustaining the earth so that life can exist. Every planet, every star, every galaxy, as well as all their energies, gravities, gasses, and elements help to some degree in creating a climate for man to exist on earth.[1]

Yet God had only one purpose in mind for this incredible creation—and that was to have you! You are not a whim of God's emotion. You have been planned since the universe began. He has chosen you as His own child.

Even the best of earthly fathers is only a type or shadow of the real thing: Father God. Nothing in the depths of our imagination could even come close to comprehending the depth of Father God's love and desire for us.

As His child, your heavenly Father loves and accepts you just as you are. There is nothing He would change, but only one thing He would add: that you might bear His resemblance!

The glorified body you will receive is the ultimate gift of a loving Father who desires to share His identity with you. It is the gift of a proud Father whom the Bible calls "papa God" (see Rom. 8:15). It is the gift of a loving Father who says without shame, "I want My kids to look like Me!" And so we shall!

What an awesome day it will be:

Behold, what manner of love the Father hath bestowed upon us, that we should be called the sons of

God: therefore the world knoweth us not, because it knew Him not.

Beloved, now are we the sons of God, and it doth not yet appear what we shall be: but we know that, when He shall appear, we shall be like Him; for we shall see Him as He is.

And every man that hath this hope in Him purifieth himself, even as He is pure.

1 John 3:1-3

Endnote

1. Hugh Ross, videotape lecture "Reasons to Believe" (P.O. Box 5978, Pasadena, CA 91117); also Hugh Ross, *Creation and Time* (Oxnard, CA: Navpress, 1994), 141.

Chapter 6

The Appearance of God and Angels

It is an awesome thing to discover how we will look and function as eternal beings. It is also exciting to learn about the appearance of God!

Jesus made an astounding statement in the Gospel of John. He said, "If you have seen Me, you have seen the Father" (see Jn. 14:9). Does that mean Father God also has a glorified body that can be seen and touched?

The question is even more significant when we consider that God the Father was not born on this planet in physical form as was His Son. The Son became flesh and dwelt among us, but what about Father God?

Likewise, God the Father never died on this earth. Does that mean God is figurative? Or is He real?

The Bible shows us more than 44 examples where God appears to man on this planet in bodily form before Jesus, a part of the Godhead, became flesh to live among us.

Here's a key illustration:

And the **Lord** *appeared unto him in the plains of Mamre: and he sat in the tent door in the heat of the day;*

And he lift up his eyes and looked, and, lo, three men stood by him: and when he saw them, he ran to meet them from the tent door, and bowed himself toward the ground,

And said, **My Lord**, *if now I have found favour in Thy sight, pass not away, I pray Thee, from Thy servant:*

Let a little water, I pray You, be fetched, and wash Your feet, and rest Yourselves under the tree:

And I will fetch a morsel of bread, and comfort Ye Your hearts; after that Ye shall pass on: for therefore are Ye come to Your servant. And they said, So do, as thou hast said.

And Abraham hastened into the tent unto Sarah, and said, Make ready quickly three measures of fine meal, knead it, and make cakes upon the hearth.

And Abraham ran unto the herd, and fetcht a calf tender and good, and gave it unto a young man; and he hasted to dress it.

And he took butter, and milk, and the calf which he had dressed, and set it before them; and he stood by them under the tree, and they did eat.

Genesis 18:1-8

In this passage, God Himself appears to Abraham "as a man." We are not saying that He is a man, but that He *looked* like a man to Abraham. Likewise, every time God appears in man's dimensions in the Scriptures, He appears as a man. That means He must have a spiritual body just as real as the physical body in which Jesus appears.

Certainly when God appears at these times, He is not appearing as God in the fulness of all of His glory and power or dimensions. Natural man wouldn't be able to handle that. Still, it is God appearing to us as a man in a body.

We can understand more from this same example in Genesis if we look at some of the Hebrew definitions. In the first verse, the word "Lord" is *Jehovah*, meaning "self-existent one, the eternal one, the one with no beginning or no end." This confirms it is indeed God Himself who, along with two angels, appears to Abraham. (Verse 1 of chapter 19 tells us the other men were angels.)

The word for "appeared" is the Hebrew word *raah*, meaning "to see, to be looked on, to show yourself, or to be viewed." Thus the eternal, self-existent God was seen by Abraham. Abraham was able to "look on" Jehovah God. If Abraham could easily look on God and those angels, it shows us how real God and the inhabitants of Heaven really are!

The verses that follow are even more wonderful. Not only do we discover that God will allow man the privilege of seeing Him, but we see that He even delights in spending the simplest of times with us!

Imagine Abraham sitting in his tent as he sees God approaching. He runs toward God and bows his face to the ground. He knows it is God; this is one of the ten times God appears to him (see Gen. 12:1,3,7; 15:1; 17; 18; 21:12; 22:1).

To say the least, Abraham is awestruck. He is in the bodily presence of Jehovah Himself, the infinite God who has no beginning or end.

After Abraham regained his composure (and it may have taken awhile), he began to fulfill the customary hospitality of his day. He fetched water and then actually washed God's feet (see Gen 18:3-5). This is a telling example of God's reality and access to us. God is touchable!

It is also a very good proof that heavenly bodies must have been similar to that of men even before Christ's birth, death, and resurrection. Most likely, heavenly bodies were similar to men's before man was ever created!

God Is Involved

As incredible as it may seem to us, Abraham then proceeded to feed God and these two angels. We even know the menu: bread, butter, milk, and veal.

The overriding message of these details is very important: God wants us to know He is real. He has a real spiritual body. With this spiritual body, you can see Him, touch Him, and wash His feet. He can eat, drink, and fellowship with you. He is not an unreal ghost or formless spirit. First Corinthians states this as plainly as possible: There are **natural bodies** and there are **spiritual bodies**. Both are incredibly real (see 1 Cor. 15:44).

Even though Jehovah is the God of the whole universe, He can and has chosen to manifest Himself to us in His heavenly body. He has done so on this planet many times.

His involvement does not stop with externals, though. When you consider the reason why He came to Abraham and his wife at Mamre, you will be even more astounded.

God's purpose was to personally start a righteous lineage through which He could redeem mankind. He already had your salvation in mind!

God promises to renew Abraham, who is 99 years old, and his wife Sarah, who is 89 years old, so that they will have a son who will start this lineage:

And they said unto him, Where is Sarah thy wife? And he said, Behold, in the tent.

And He said, I will certainly return unto thee according to the time of life; and, lo, Sarah thy wife shall have a son. And Sarah heard it in the tent door, which was behind Him.

Now Abraham and Sarah were old and well stricken in age; and it ceased to be with Sarah after the manner of women.

Therefore Sarah laughed within herself, saying, After I am waxed old shall I have pleasure, my lord being old also?

And the Lord said unto Abraham, Wherefore did Sarah laugh, saying, Shall I of a surety bear a child, which am old?

Is any thing too hard for the Lord? At the time appointed I will return unto thee, according to the time of life, and Sarah shall have a son.

Then Sarah denied, saying, I laughed not; for she was afraid. And He said, Nay; but thou didst laugh.

Genesis 18:9-15

"Lineage" in this context means a "line of people, a descendent line, a bloodline."

We know God's intention came to pass, for a year later Isaac was miraculously born to Abraham and Sarah. The message that this encounter tells us is that God considered man's redemption to be so important that He left nothing to chance. He chose no man or angel for this task. God Himself appeared in person to begin this lineage some 2,348 years before Christ.

In the same way, God personally fulfilled the need of a sacrifice to die for man's sin. He miraculously incarnated in the flesh as Jesus Christ to be born of a virgin. He became a man in the form of Christ to die for us—finishing all He had begun.

We must remember, though, that Jesus' birth was not His beginning point. Jesus had always existed in eternity. Yet in order to come forth in the righteous lineage God intended, He clothed Himself with flesh to live among us. The angels called Him "Emmanuel," or "God is with us."

The real reason God left His throne in glory to appear as a man was for your benefit. The same God who created a universe that could sustain your life on earth also came in a body to Abraham to guarantee your part in His lineage! He left that mission to no one else!

Then more than 2,000 years later, He appeared again through Christ in that lineage to personally pay for your right of entrance into Heaven.

He Knows You

A God who loves this much does much to show His care. The verses that follow show us that God is intensely personal.

In this passage, the angels have gone on a mission to Sodom and Gomorrah, leaving God and Abraham alone:

> *And the men rose up from thence, and looked toward Sodom: and Abraham went with them to bring them on the way.*
>
> *And the Lord said, Shall I hide from Abraham that thing which I do;*
>
> *Seeing that Abraham shall surely become a great and mighty nation, and all the nations of the earth shall be blessed in him?*
>
> *For I know him, that he will command his children and his household after him, and they shall keep the way of the Lord, to do justice and judgment; that the Lord may bring upon Abraham that which He hath spoken of him.*
>
> *And the Lord said, Because the cry of Sodom and Gomorrah is great, and because their sin is very grievous;*
>
> *I will go down now, and see whether they have done altogether according to the cry of it, which is come unto Me; and if not, I will know.*
>
> *And the men turned their faces from thence, and went toward Sodom: but Abraham stood yet before the Lord.*
>
> Genesis 18:16-22

God is considering the heavy matter of the destruction of Sodom and Gomorrah for their great sin. He weighs what part Abraham might play in a solution for the dilemma.

And Abraham drew near, and said, Wilt Thou also destroy the righteous with the wicked?

Peradventure there be fifty righteous within the city: wilt Thou also destroy and not spare the place for the fifty righteous that are therein?

That be far from Thee to do after this manner, to slay the righteous with the wicked: and that the righteous should be as the wicked, that be far from Thee: Shall not the Judge of all the earth do right?

And the Lord said, If I find in Sodom fifty righteous within the city, then I will spare all the place for their sakes.

Genesis 18:23-26

The Scriptures say that Abraham "drew up close to God" and began to intercede for Sodom and Gomorrah. Abraham was greatly concerned, for his nephew, Lot, lived there with his family.

In this conversation, we see the concerned, loving heart of Father God as He patiently listens to His son, Abraham. He is giving great attention to what concerns His son. Abraham experiences the joy of a son who has his Father's undivided attention, and the worth of a son whose Father treats him with great importance. He continues:

And Abraham answered and said, Behold now, I have taken upon me to speak unto the Lord, which am but dust and ashes:

Peradventure there shall lack five of the fifty righteous: wilt Thou destroy all the city for lack of five? And He said, If I find there forty and five, I will not destroy it.

And he spake unto Him yet again, and said, Peradventure there shall be forty found there. And He said, I will not do it for forty's sake.

And he said unto Him, Oh let not the Lord be angry, and I will speak: Peradventure there shall be thirty found there. And He said, I will not do it, if I find thirty there.

And he said, Behold now, I have taken upon me to speak unto the Lord: Peradventure there shall be twenty found there. And He said, I will not destroy it for twenty's sake.

And he said, Oh let not the Lord be angry, and I will speak yet but this once: Peradventure ten shall be found there. And He said, I will not destroy it for ten's sake.

And the Lord went His way, as soon as He had left communing with Abraham: and Abraham returned unto his place.

Genesis 18:27-33

What is truly great about these verses is that Abraham was not enlightening God in any way. God was fully aware of the situation in Sodom and did not want to destroy the righteous along with the wicked. God actually chose to tell Abraham about the situation because He knew that Abraham would intercede on Sodom's behalf. This is just what God intended all along.

Abraham's intervention pictured at the start of a lineage what would happen at the end of the line. Jesus, God's own Son, would intervene once and for all so that the righteous would not be destroyed along with the wicked. More than 2,348 years before it happened, God gave us a model of His ultimate and personal plan of saving intervention for His children.

A God You Can Touch

Throughout this chapter of Genesis are timeless and incredible truths about our God. We see that long before Christ ever appeared, God was seen in our dimension in a body. He ate and drank, was seen and touched, and even had His feet washed.

We see a personal God who wants to reveal His purpose and secrets to us. He told Abraham His plans, allowing him to take part in the righteous solution.

These are not just examples from thousands of years ago, but markers of eternal truths of a God who is the same today, yesterday, and forever (see Heb. 13:8). God wants you to ask Him for what you desire. God will listen to your plans.

God longs to relate to us as our Father. He desires to spend time with us. He patiently attends to our concerns. It must have taken Abraham hours to kill a calf, dress it, and cook it. Yet God didn't seem to mind. He sat and talked with Abraham, His son and His friend.

This same God longs for that intimacy with you, every day.

You Are His Personal Image

There are other proofs of a personal God appearing to His sons.

In the Old Testament, God appeared to Adam in Genesis. It says that God would come and walk with Adam in the garden in the cool of the day (see Gen. 3:8).

Adam wasn't walking with a ghost, or a figurative mist. God was real and had a real spiritual body. In fact, the heavenly body of God is the pattern from which Adam was made.

Genesis tells us, "And God said, Let Us make man in Our image, after Our likeness..." (Gen. 1:26). The Hebrew word for "image" is *tselem*, meaning a "representative," or to "shade something." It literally means "a shadow."

Tselem actually paints a picture of how God created man. God stood in the Garden of Eden and allowed His shadow to fall upon the ground. He then shaped man into the form of His own shadow!

The Scriptures say He "formed" man from the dust of the ground (see Gen. 2:7). "Formed" is the Hebrew word *yatsor*, meaning "to squeeze into shape like a potter does with clay." God squeezed the clay into His shadow. He made His shadow! (Of course, God has to be real to have a shadow!)

Similarly, the word for "likeness" is the Hebrew *demuwth*, meaning "to model, fashion, resemble." Quite simply, God allowed His shadow to become the pattern for creating man. He then fashioned man to resemble Himself. He did all this that man might have fellowship with Him—and that man might be like Him.

God and Adam had that fellowship. They walked together in the beautiful garden in the cool of the day and God taught Adam about life. He's a very personal God who wants to be seen by man and have close relationship with him.

In Exodus, we are told that Moses and God spoke face to face. "And the Lord spake unto Moses face to face, as a man speaketh unto his friend" (Ex. 33:11a). Moses saw God. They looked at each other face to face, and they talked face to face. That's quite personal!

Some may be confused by the verse that says "no man can see God's face and live" (see Ex. 33:20). Understanding the context of the verse will clarify any confusion. For too long, the enemy of our souls has tried to paint God as a faceless spirit—to disguise Him and limit our access and understanding of a God who is real.

After Moses and the Lord talked together as friends, Moses asked God, "God, show me Your glory. Let me see You in Your glory" (see Ex. 33:18). Moses had enjoyed seeing God in His bodily dimensions, but now he was asking God to let Himself be seen in His own glorious dimensions.

Moffatt's translation of this same verse reads, "Let me see Thy majesty." This would mean the fullness of His glory! God does not rebuke Moses for asking. He simply says, "I can't, Moses. You couldn't see Me in all My dimensions—in the fullness of My glory—and live."

Yet this same loving God says, in effect, "I'll tell you what I'll do, though. I'll put you in the cleft of a rock and I'll put My hand over you when I pass by. I'll let you look at

My back as I move away. But My face, in its glory, you cannot see."

We know that Moses actually saw the back of God's heavenly body, His body of glory (see Ex. 33:20-23). That in itself was enough to light up Moses' face with so much glory that he had to cover it with a cloth (see Ex. 34:29-35).

There are approximately 44 other times that God appears to man in Scripture. For example, Joshua saw the Lord (see Josh. 5:13-15). Elijah saw Him (see 1 Kings 19). He was seen by Isaiah (see Is. 6). Job saw the Lord (see Job 42:5). Amos saw the Lord standing upon the altar (see Amos 9:1). Every verse underscores that the inhabitants of Heaven and God Himself have real, heavenly bodies.

Whenever God did appear to man on earth, we know that He had to vastly humble Himself to come into our dimension. Thank God there is a day coming when we shall see Him in all His glory!

Like Jesus

Can we be any more specific about God's appearance? The Gospel of John surely helps:

> *Let not your heart be troubled: ye believe in God, believe also in Me.*
>
> *In My Father's house are many mansions: if it were not so, I would have told you. I go to prepare a place for you.*
>
> *And if I go and prepare a place for you, I will come again, and receive you unto Myself; that where I am, there ye may be also.*

And whither I go ye know, and the way ye know.

Thomas saith unto Him, Lord, we know not whither Thou goest; and how can we know the way?

Jesus saith unto him, I am the way, the truth, and the life: no man cometh unto the Father, but by Me.

If ye had known Me, ye should have known My Father also: and from ***henceforth ye know Him, and have seen Him.***

Philip saith unto Him, Lord, shew us the Father, and it sufficeth us.

Jesus saith unto him, Have I been so long time with you, and yet hast thou not known Me, Philip? he that hath seen Me hath seen the Father; and how sayest thou then, Shew us the Father?

Believest thou not that I am in the Father, and the Father in Me? *the words that I speak unto you I speak not of Myself: but the Father that dwelleth in Me, He doeth the works.*

Believe Me that I am in the Father, and the Father in Me: or else believe Me for the very works' sake.

John 14:1-11

According to the Scriptures, God looks like Jesus! Jesus made it clear that if you'd seen Him, you had seen the Father. We are not going to worship some figurative being that cannot be seen throughout eternity. He's visibly, tangibly real, and Jesus put a face on God for us.

This makes the Book of Colossians come alive when it says that Jesus "is the image of the invisible God" (Col. 1:15).

"Image" in Greek is *eikon*, meaning "striking resemblance." The 20th Century New Testament says, "He is the very incarnation of God." William's translation says, "He is the exact likeness of God." Knox's translation reads, "Jesus is the true likeness of a God we cannot see." The Amplified Bible states, "[Now] He is the exact likeness of the unseen God [the visible representation of the invisible]; He is the Firstborn of all creation."

That sounds clear: God looks like Jesus! The Holy Spirit looks like Jesus. Jesus said, "He's My other self" (see Jn. 14:16). Thus the Godhead looks like Jesus! They are three in one: the Trinity. They have distinct personalities, but a common image!

Angels

Angels are some of the most talked about heavenly beings. The Scriptures are not silent concerning their appearance or function, either.

According to the Word, angels are not those who have died in Christ. They are a separate creation of God sent to minister to the needs of the believer:

> *But to which of the angels said He at any time, Sit on My right hand, until I make thine enemies thy footstool?*
>
> *Are they not all ministering spirits, sent forth to minister for them who shall be heirs of salvation?*
>
> Hebrews 1:13-14

The same account we reviewed in Genesis speaks of two angels who also appear as men to Abraham, and then depart to do the work they had been assigned in Sodom.

That example makes it clear that angels also can appear as men in our dimensions of length, breadth, height, and space.

In fact, according to the Book of Hebrews, they can appear so similar to men that we cannot tell them apart:

Let brotherly love continue.

Be not forgetful to entertain strangers: for thereby some have ***entertained angels unawares.***

Hebrews 13:1-2

Goodspeed's translation of this verse says, "Some have without knowing it had angels as their guest."

It seems an angel would have to look very similar to a man for you to entertain one and not be aware of it! In fact, seeing an angel in this manner may be more common than we know.

Another way angels appear is in their glorified bodies, with wings (see Ex. 25:20; Ezek. 1:23-25). Though their appearances are infrequent and awesome, it does not kill us to see angels in this state. Their glory is brilliant, yet still far less than that of God.

Heavenly Beings Made Real

What a privilege to "de-mystify" Heaven and find out how real the inhabitants are!

God is real; you can see Him. Angels are real; you can see them. Jesus is real; you can see Him. You may not see them in this lifetime, but it is possible. You will see them for sure in Heaven!

You will also see every person who has ever died in Christ. Their glorified bodies are very real. Words fail to describe all the splendor of Heaven's realities. For the time being we are left to "groan" while we wait for the revelation! (See Romans 8:22-23.) Yet the day approaches when we will live in the eternal, magnificent, visible presence of God and all He has made!

Chapter 7

Eternal Things

What God does, He does forever (see Eccles. 3:14). He has planned for all eternity how we shall be like Him, and how our bodies shall take on His eternal form.

And He hasn't kept it a secret!

Imagine how our frail, earthly bodies will be made to last forever. Imagine life beyond the pains and limitations of our earthly "shells." We shall become incorruptible!

> *So also is the resurrection of the dead. It is sown in corruption;* ***it is raised in incorruption:***
>
> *It is sown in dishonour; it is raised in glory: it is sown in weakness; it is raised in power:*
>
> *It is sown a natural body; it is raised a spiritual body. There is a natural body, and there is a spiritual body.*
>
> *And so it is written, The first man Adam was made a living soul; the last Adam was made a quickening spirit.*
>
> *Howbeit that was not first which is spiritual, but that which is natural; and afterward that which is spiritual.*

The first man is of the earth, earthy: the second man is the Lord from heaven.

As is the earthy, such are they also that are earthy: and as is the heavenly, such are they also that are heavenly.

And as we have borne the image of the earthy, we shall also bear the image of the heavenly.

Now this I say, brethren, that ***flesh and blood cannot inherit the kingdom of God****; neither doth corruption inherit incorruption.*

Behold, I shew you a mystery; We shall not all sleep, but we shall all be changed,

In a moment, in the twinkling of an eye, at the last trump: for the trumpet shall sound, and the dead shall be raised incorruptible, and we shall be changed.

1 Corinthians 15:42-52

How exactly do we become incorruptible? How can we escape "time" as we know it? The answers are subtle, but we can find them in the Scriptures.

The first deals with our own flesh. Notice the verse we quoted in First Corinthians that says, "flesh and *blood* cannot inherit the kingdom of God." This verse becomes key with the insight Jesus gave to His disciples after His resurrection. Note this verse does not say "flesh and *bone* cannot inherit the kingdom of God."

You'll discover there is a vast difference between the two. In fact, it is the difference between the substance of our heavenly and earthly bodies!

Consider the following passage in Luke. Jesus had already appeared to the two men on the road to Emmaus after His resurrection. The men went to tell Christ's disciples about His appearing to them. As the group talked, Jesus came to them—right through the wall.

And as they thus spake, Jesus Himself stood in the midst of them, and saith unto them, Peace be unto you.

But they were terrified and affrighted, and supposed that they had seen a spirit.

And He said unto them, Why are ye troubled? and why do thoughts arise in your hearts?

Behold My hands and My feet, that it is I Myself: handle Me, and see; ***for a spirit hath not flesh and bones, as ye see Me have.***

And when He had thus spoken, He shewed them His hands and His feet.

And while they yet believed not for joy, and wondered, He said unto them, Have ye here any meat?

And they gave Him a piece of broiled fish, and of an honeycomb.

And He took it, and did eat before them.

And He said unto them, These are the words which I spake unto you, while I was yet with you, that all things must be fulfilled, which were written in the law of Moses, and in the prophets, and in the psalms, concerning Me.

Then opened He their understanding, that they might understand the scriptures,

And said unto them, Thus it is written, and thus it behoved Christ to suffer, and to rise from the dead the third day.

Luke 24:36-46

Carefully note that Jesus says, "A spirit hath not flesh and *bones*, as ye see Me have." Note the omission of the *blood*. You can still see and touch Jesus. He has flesh and bones, but no blood.

His glorified body did not have any blood in it. Jesus had already shed His blood on Calvary and taken every drop of it into Heaven and applied it to the mercy seat for man's sin.

If our glorified bodies are fashioned like His (see Phil. 3:21), then we too will have flesh and bone, but no blood.

There are many other scriptural clues to support this. Leviticus 17:11 says, "For the life of the flesh is in the blood." It speaks of life in this dimension. Medical science knows this now, even though Moses proclaimed it more than 3,000 years ago.

Blood is not needed to sustain life in the glorified state; God has something far superior to pulsate eternal life within us.

Sustained by His Glory

The means for sustaining our eternal life appears to be God's *glory* itself. God's glory manifested as brilliant light or brightness appears to be the eternal power we need to produce life itself in our flesh and bones.

If this is true, then His very essence will infuse us and flow through us like electricity through the wires of a building. We will constantly be energized by Him forever!

A multitude of Scriptures bear witness to this. Philippians says:

> [He] *shall change our vile body, that it may be fashioned like unto His glorious body....*
>
> Philippians 3:21

"Glorious" in the Greek is *doxa*, or "all that is good in God." It comprises all that God will be in His final revelation to us...His self-revelation...His brilliance...His brightness... His splendor...His *light.*

God's glory often appears in the Scriptures as light. In Luke, some shepherds in a field saw the angel of the Lord. It says that "the glory of the Lord shone round about them" (Lk. 2:9).

"Glory" in this example is also *doxa*. It says that *doxa* shone round about them. "Shone round about" is translated from the Greek word *perilampo*, with *peri*, meaning "through" and "around"; and *lampo*, meaning "to illuminate." Thus, *perilampo* is to illuminate all around.

Our English word *lamp* comes from this word. A lamp illuminates the area all around it. Electric energy flows and the lamp shines "round about."

In the case of the shepherds, the glory of the Lord illuminated the night sky all around them. God's glory manifested itself as light or brightness.

Another important example can be found in the Gospel of John. These verses speak of God's eternal existence as light.

Seeing this relationship gives us more insight into how we too become eternal.

In the beginning was the Word, and the Word was with God, and the Word was God.

The same was in the beginning with God.

All things were made by Him; and without Him was not any thing made that was made.

In Him was life; and the life was the ***light*** *of men.*

And the light shineth in darkness; and the darkness comprehended it not.

There was a man sent from God, whose name was John.

The same came for a witness, to bear witness of the ***Light****, that all men through him might believe.*

He was not that Light, but was sent to bear witness of that Light.

That was the true Light, which lighteth every man that cometh into the world.

He was in the world, and the world was made by Him, and the world knew Him not.

He came unto His own, and His own received Him not.

But as many as received Him, to them gave He power to become the sons of God, even to them that believe on His name:

Which were born, not of blood, nor of the will of the flesh, nor of the will of man, but of God.

And the Word was made flesh, and dwelt among us, ***(and we beheld His glory****, the glory as of the only begotten of the Father,) full of grace and truth.*

John 1:1-14

Other verses note the same parallel. Speaking of Christ, Isaiah prophesies:

The people that walked in darkness have seen a great ***light....***

Isaiah 9:2

Jesus Himself said:

...I am the ***light*** *of the world....*

John 8:12

Of God's creation, it is spoken:

For God, who commanded the ***light*** *to shine out of darkness....*

2 Corinthians 4:6

Speaking of God Himself, John says:

This then is the message which we have heard of Him, and declare unto you, that God is ***light****, and in Him is no darkness at all.*

1 John 1:5

A reference to Heaven tells us:

And the city had no need of the sun, neither of the moon, to shine it it: for the ***glory*** *of God did lighten it, and the Lamb is the* ***light*** *thereof.*

Revelation 21:23

Understanding that God is light is the key to helping us see how our natural, blood-filled bodies can escape decay. Let's look at the science of light to better appreciate this concept and to discover how we might enter a timeless, or eternal, dimension.

The Science of Light

It is a scientific fact that light travels at a speed of 186,272 miles per second. That means light travels six million million miles, or a total of 5.88 trillion miles, in one year!

To understand the vast size of our universe, consider this: It would take more than 100 million years at the speed of light to travel from one end of the Milky Way to the other.

It is impossible to fathom these numbers. It has been said that if you wound an old alarm clock and counted every tick and tock, it would take 32,000 years to reach one million million. Yet light travels at a speed of six million million miles every year.

In one hour's time, light travels 670 million miles. To grasp the speed of light, imagine firing a rifle whose bullet could travel at the speed of light. That bullet would travel around the circumference of the earth seven times before you could get your finger off the trigger! It would travel around the earth at least twice before you heard the explosion!

These concepts are quite relevant when you consider time and eternity. It is known that the faster you go, the closer you come to the eternal dimension—because time actually slows down. Scientists call this the time dilation theory. It is based on Einstein's general law of relativity ($E=mc^2$).

This means that if you traveled in a spaceship at 87% of the speed of light, time (for you) would slow down by 50%. For example, if you left earth when you were 25 years old and traveled at 87% of the speed of light for 50 years, when you returned, you would have aged only 25 years rather than

50 years. Everyone who was 25 years old like you when you left would now be 75! Yet you would only be 50. Time for you would have slowed down by 50%.

Scientists have proven this to be true by the use of special clocks that have been sent into space. The first clock was sent in John Glenn's space capsule. After orbiting the earth for about three hours at a speed of only 18,000 miles per hour, his space clock recorded a time difference. John Glenn returned to earth 1/10,000 of a second younger than if he had not left earth.[1]

Although that may not seem like a significant amount, the difference is staggering if you accelerate to the speed of light: 186,272 miles per second.

If you were to travel at 99.99% of the speed of light, and you traveled in outer space for 60 years at that speed, when you returned to earth you would discover that five million years had passed by!

The logical conclusion is that if you could travel at 100% of the speed of light, time as we know it would stop. The moment "now" would become "forever"...and you would enter eternity. You would enter ageless time!

Ageless Time

Knowing that God *is* light means that the moment "now" for God is forever. God is eternal, and time has absolutely no hold on Him. He created time so that man might live in it, but He only made so much of it. We are running out of time as we know it.

For God, this poses no problem. He is not a created being, so He has no beginning and will have no end. He is not bound by time or time's dimensions. He can go forward or backward in time. His Word says that He sees the end from the beginning. He is the First and the Last, the Alpha and Omega; before the beginning of time and continuing after it ends.

To demonstrate this, picture a time line. Time as we know it has three dimensions in which we regularly operate. (As we have discussed before, there may be at least 8 more dimensions for God since we know of at least 11 existing dimensions, according to particle physics.)

Our three simple dimensions are past, present, and future.

We can only move in one direction on this time line, and that is forward. God, on the other hand, sits outside of time and can operate in all its dimensions. He sees the past, present, and future the same; all are easily accessible to Him. God can see Adam and Eve, the apostles, and us at the same time. He also can separate any aspect of time whenever He so desires. He does the same in considering your own life as well.

The fact that God is light, that He is eternal, and that He is not bound by time helps explain the change He can make in our bodies so that they too can become eternal.

If our glorified bodies are flesh and bone without blood, and most likely light, then we can better understand how we could become timeless.

At the speed of light we enter into eternity, and time as we know it stops. It follows, then, that as God's glory fills our glorified bodies, we too become timeless.

For years Bible scholars have believed that our body composition would take on some form of light, for that is implied within the word *glorified.*

Yet only in recent years has it been discovered that the elements in blood are quite similar to the elements in light. Some theorists have even called blood "liquid light." Blood in our physical bodies serves as a model for us of how light or "glory" will be in our glorified bodies.

Blood and Light

Some of these aspects of blood and light can be found in the book, *The Chemistry of the Blood*, by M.R. DeHaan, M.D. Dr. DeHaan's observations are noted first (the emphasis is added), with our parallels following:

> "The human body has many kinds of tissues...muscle, nerve, fat, glands, bone, etc. All these tissues have one thing in common: they are fixed cells, microscopically small and having a specific and limited function. Unlike these fixed tissues, *the blood is fluid and mobile, that is, it is not limited to one part of the body but is free to move throughout the entire body to supply all fixed cells....*"[2]

Similarly, light has a fluid quality that allows it to circulate, fill, and nourish! The ability to reach every place in the body is not easily accomplished—yet can readily be done by a liquid such as blood and the similar "fluidity" found in light.

> "The blood is the most mysterious of all tissues, being composed of scores of elements and compounds and

strange chemical bodies, whose function is not yet fully understood, but all of which have to do with the mystery of life, for the life...is in the blood. Once the blood fails to reach the cells and members of the body, they promptly die and no man ever dies until his blood ceases to circulate."[3]

The qualities of light are similar. Consider the process of photosynthesis, and the life given from exposure to light. Think of the chemical composition change that happens during the process. Think of the death that would occur on earth without the light of the sun, and how mysteriously it provides its life-giving forces.

"The blood consists mainly of three kinds of cells: platelets, erythrocytes, and leucocytes."[4]

"There are three main kinds of light rays: chemical or actinic rays, light rays, and heat rays."[5]

The two appear to have a lot in common!

Certainly a more exhaustive scientific study would yield more proofs. Yet the parallels are obvious; and the similar schemes throughout God's marvelous creation are a joy to discover!

Though we don't exactly know how it will happen, the fact remains that we shall be changed. We shall become eternal and leave this earth in the twinkling of an eye!

An Atomic Second

Understanding the speed of light helps us answer another question.

How will we leave this earth in the "twinkling of an eye"?

According to First Corinthians, that is the promise for every person in Christ on the day of the rapture (see 1 Cor. 15:52).

That kind of speed is very fast! The Greek word for "twinkling" in this verse is *atomo*, from which we get our English words *atom* and *atomic.*

Quite simply, that means one instant we will be here, and the next instant we'll be gone. Of course, our physical bodies could not withstand that kind of speed. They would implode.

How do we transcend that challenge? Again, timelessness is central to our new eternal nature.

If we are changed to be fashioned like unto Christ's glorious body, and we see that the glory of the Lord is light, then we too would take on His timeless composition. We would enter the eternal dimension where we will be forever with Him.

In order to accurately make this departure in a mere second of time, we would have to leave this earth at a minimum speed of at least 186,272 miles per second—the speed of light! How else could we be immediately present with the Lord?

> *...To be absent from the body, and to be present with the Lord.*
>
> 2 Corinthians 5:8

Even at the speed of light, getting to Heaven would take some time. Surely it is not beyond God's scope for us to travel even faster. Some assert that God moves at "thought speed." As fast as you think it, you are there. Perhaps it is so.

Today scientists are discovering other ways to travel faster and skip entire galaxies. If man can discover this with his finite mind, how much more can our God do?

Consider the computer concept of using "windows" to skip reviewing whole subsystems of information.

Space scientists make use of the same concept through what are known as "folds in space"; "worm holes"; "tunnels"; and "windows." To gain entrance to certain portions of space, NASA specialists already know they must go through certain "windows" and that they must carefully schedule their time coordinates to insure direct access to them.[6]

In effect, this means you need not travel only at the speed of light, but you could "warp" or skip directly to where you need to be in another galaxy.

People who have died and come back to life frequently report passing through a series of "tunnels" of light and being immediately in the presence of God...and those without God report seeing tunnels of incredible darkness. Certainly this is food for thought!

If it sounds beyond our comprehension, we must simply remember with whom we are dealing! God has created eternal things—of which we are foremost—and there is nothing too hard for our God!

Endnotes

1. Hugh Ross, videotape lecture "Reasons to Believe" (P.O. Box 5978, Pasadena, CA 91117).

2. M.R. DeHaan, M.D., *The Chemistry of the Blood* (Grand Rapids, MI: Lamplighter Books, Zondervan Publishing House, 1943), 14.

3. DeHaan, *The Chemistry of the Blood*, 14-15.

4. DeHaan, *The Chemistry of the Blood*, 18-19.

5. DeHaan, *The Chemistry of the Blood*, 62.

6. Stephen W. Hawking, *A Brief History of Time* (Toronto: Bantam Books, 1988), 89.

Chapter 8

The Great Cloud of Witnesses

We've seen the reality of a place called Heaven. We've learned much about the real, eternal beings who live there. We've considered how we will be gloriously changed to be like Jesus.

Now let's take an inside look at the inhabitants of Heaven...and what they know.

No doubt you have lost a loved one in death or know someone who has. You may have wondered if your glorified loved ones know what is going on here on earth. Do they follow your activities? Do they know about your children or your life?

You've probably heard someone say that "so-and-so is looking down from Heaven." Is that wishful thinking, or is there evidence to suggest it is true?

Frankly, the Bible has much to tell us about what the inhabitants of Heaven know.

The following text from Luke is a great start. This is the account of Christ's transfiguration before His disciples, and the appearance of two men on earth who were actually residents of Heaven:

> *And it came to pass about an eight days after these sayings, He took Peter and John and James, and went up into a mountain to pray.*
>
> *And as He prayed, the fashion of His countenance was altered, and His raiment was white and glistering.*
>
> *And, behold, there talked with Him two men,* ***which were Moses and Elias****:*
>
> *Who appeared in glory, and spake of His decease which He should accomplish at Jerusalem.*
>
> *But Peter and they that were with him were heavy with sleep: and when they were awake, they saw His glory, and the two men that stood with Him.*
>
> *And it came to pass, as they departed from Him, Peter said unto Jesus, Master, it is good for us to be here: and let us make three tabernacles; one for Thee, and one for Moses, and one for Elias: not knowing what he said.*
>
> *While he thus spake, there came a cloud, and overshadowed them: and they feared as they entered into the cloud.*
>
> *And there came a voice out of the cloud, saying, This is My beloved Son: hear Him.*
>
> *And when the voice was past, Jesus was found alone. And they kept it close, and told no man in those day any of those things which they had seen.*
>
> Luke 9:28-36

As Jesus prayed and Peter, John, and James dozed, God's glory bursts down upon them and Jesus is transfigured.

(As we have noted before, God's presence is light. It says literally that God's glory, *perilampo*, "shone round about them" just as happened to the shepherds in the field when the angels announced the birth of Christ.)

Jesus' face shone as the sun and His clothing became white as the light. At the same moment this flash of glory happened, two men appeared. According to God's Word, these men were Moses and Elias (Elijah)—residents of Heaven!

Moses had died hundreds of years before this event. Elijah had not died, but had simply been caught up to Heaven in a whirlwind also hundreds of years earlier. Both had been inhabitants of Heaven for a great length of time.

Now they appear to Jesus, Peter, James, and John here on earth. Note that they looked like men, and that they appeared in the brilliant "light of God" or *doxa* (verses 30-31).

It is the context of their conversation that is most significant, however. Moses and Elijah had a specific purpose in speaking with Jesus; they talked to Him about His mission on earth and forthcoming death in Jerusalem.

The J.B. Phillips translation of Greek to modern English says, "They talked of the way He must take and the end He must fulfill." Berkeley's translation states, "They talked about His exodus."

Here we find two residents of Heaven who had already experienced their own unique exodus from the earth. Now they speak to Christ about His own upcoming exodus—to give Him strength.

They were giving Him courage to run the race set before Him:

> *Wherefore seeing we also are compassed about with so great a cloud of witnesses, let us lay aside every weight, and the sin which doth so easily beset us, and let us run with patience the race that is set before us,*
>
> *Looking unto Jesus the author and finisher of our faith....*
>
> Hebrews 12:1-2

Simply put, we are surrounded by a host of heavenly witnesses, like Moses and Elijah, who do see and know what we do to run our race of faith!

The New English Bible says, "They discussed His departure and the destiny He was to fulfill" (Lk. 9:31). These witnesses knew about Jesus' destiny. They knew about His race and what He faced. They knew in detail His mission on the earth and what was planned for Him in Jerusalem.

That is why their discussion was quite specific and purposeful. Moses and Elijah didn't talk about Heaven or how great it is. They did not discuss streets of gold, gates of pearl, thrones of sapphire, or eternal praise. *It is very significant that they discussed what events were taking place on earth that had great spiritual impact.* And they could only talk about it if they *knew* that information!

Kingdom Business

Thus it seems departed saints do know what is happening now in God's Kingdom on earth. They seem to be very much aware of what is taking place in our spiritual progress. In fact, according to Scripture, they follow this progress with great interest:

> *There was a certain rich man, which was clothed in purple and fine linen, and fared sumptuously every day:*
>
> *And there was a certain beggar named Lazarus, which was laid at his gate, full of sores,*
>
> *And desiring to be fed with the crumbs which fell from the rich man's table: moreover the dogs came and licked his sores.*
>
> *And it came to pass, that the beggar died, and was carried by the angels into Abraham's bosom: the rich man also died, and was buried;*
>
> *And in hell he lift up his eyes, being in torments, and seeth Abraham afar off, and Lazarus in his bosom.*
>
> *And he cried and said, Father Abraham, have mercy on me, and send Lazarus, that he may dip the tip of his finger in water, and cool my tongue; for I am tormented in this flame.*
>
> *But Abraham said, Son, remember that thou in thy lifetime receivedst thy good things, and likewise Lazarus evil things: but now he is comforted, and thou art tormented.*
>
> *And beside all this, between us and you there is a great gulf fixed: so that they which would pass from hence to you cannot; neither can they pass to us, that would come from thence.*

Then he said, I pray thee therefore, father, that thou wouldest send him to my father's house:

For I have five brethren; that he may testify unto them, lest they also come into this place of torment.

Abraham saith unto him, They have Moses and the prophets; let them hear them.

And he said, Nay, father Abraham: but if one went unto them from the dead, they will repent.

And he said unto him, If they hear not Moses and the prophets, neither will they be persuaded, though one rose from the dead.

Luke 16:19-31

This passage is summed up well by Dake's Annotated Reference Bible: "It is the story of two beggars: one who begged in this life, and the other who begged in the next life."[1]

Most likely this story is not a parable because Jesus used real names in giving this account. It appears to be a true story about an event that happened. Jesus used it to illustrate the consciousness of people both in Heaven and hell—and their awareness of what is going on here on earth.

The rich man in hell and Abraham in paradise both knew what was happening on earth. (Notice also that the rich man easily recognized Lazarus, the beggar he had known on earth.)

As the rich man and Abraham talked, they both knew what was happening at the house of the rich man's father. They knew that five brothers of the rich man had not yet turned to God. They both knew the five were headed for hell. The rich man, in the midst of his own distress, was so concerned for his brothers that he begged Abraham to send someone to warn them.

The rich man beseeched Abraham to send someone "lest they also come into this place of torment" (verse 28). Abraham essentially said, "If they don't believe the Word of the Lord already abundantly released on earth, then they won't believe it if someone rose from the dead—just like you didn't believe it, either."

The amazing evidence is that Abraham and the rich man, who had both died and gone to Heaven and hell respectively, both knew what was happening on earth to some degree.

It also appears that one of the torments of hell is knowing and watching others you love following in your footsteps of rebellion to God and joining you in hell. At that point, there is nothing you can do....

The Purpose of Such Knowledge

Biblical insight does not suggest that departed saints watch every detail of our lives. We have no proof that they are concerned with the "day to day" or trivial aspects of our lives, such as what we are wearing or where we go.

Yet it does appear that these glorified godly ones do know and concern themselves with major events and the spiritual progress in our lives. Their most important interests seem to be salvation and the fulfillment of our God-given purpose on the earth.

They are "heavenly minded" in their focus:

> *The first man [was] from out of earth, made of dust (earthly-minded); the second Man [is] the Lord from out of heaven.*
>
> *Now those who are made of the dust are like him who was first made of the dust (earthly-minded); and as is [the Man] from heaven, so also [are those] who are of heaven (heavenly-minded).*
>
> 1 Corinthians 15:47-48 AMP

Scores of personal testimonies attest to this concept. One is that of Dr. Kenneth Hagin, which he recalls in his *Word of Faith* Magazine.[2]

Dr. Hagin tells about his only sister who died of cancer at the young age of 55. The morning after she died, he lay in his bed thinking about the time his own heart stopped when he was deathly ill in 1933. He recalled how his spirit had left his body, and how he had looked back down and seen his body lying there while his mother held his hand.

As he thought about his sister dying, he thought how she must have looked down and seen him and her loved ones gathered around her bed in love and concern.

Dr. Hagin's account is very clear as he remembers that right in the middle of his thoughts:

> "Suddenly, a beam of light from heaven about as big as an elevator shaft penetrated right through the ceiling. When that light touched me, my spirit left my body and went right up through that beam of light as if I were going up an elevator until I reached heaven.
>
> "As soon as I reached heaven, I saw my sister talking to Jesus. When I walked up to them, Jesus stopped talking to her, and my sister turned around and saw me.

"My sister said several things to me as we stood there talking. I won't go into all that she talked to me about, but among other things she said, 'I saw Ann.' [Ann was her daughter who had died as a result of an automobile accident when she was only 25 years old, leaving two small children.]

"My sister continued, 'The first thing Ann said to me was, "How are Bill and the children?" [Bill was Ann's husband.] I didn't tell Ann that Bill had remarried. People up here are not interested in the natural side of life. They are not concerned about whether or not you bought a new dress or a new suit, or how much money you have in the bank. They are concerned about spiritual things. They know what you do spiritually. They know when you make a decision for Christ.'

"My sister was talking about the cloud of witnesses in heaven who are watching us run the spiritual race that is set before us."

Dr. Hagin continues to say that his sister implored him to talk to her youngest son who was running from God. She requested that he tell her son that his life would never go right until he returned to the Lord, and that she would know when he did. Hagin concludes by saying her son did rededicate his life to God...something over which we know both Ann and the angels rejoiced! (See Luke 15:10.)

Rest assured then, that those who have gone on before us are indeed filled with wonderful and purposeful knowledge to the end that God's purposes might be fulfilled!

So Great a Cloud...and You

Remember that these heavenly witnesses have in their mind to encourage you!

What a motivation to know that those who have already run their race to inherit a "better and an enduring substance" in Heaven are personally urging you to do the same!

> *Wherefore seeing we also are compassed about with so great a cloud of witnesses, let us lay aside every weight, and the sin which doth so easily beset us, and let us run with patience the race that is set before us,*
>
> *Looking unto Jesus the author and finisher of our faith....*
>
> Hebrews 12:1-2

Those witnesses include all your departed loved ones—family and friends—and the very greatest men and women of faith of whom the Bible ever records! Your witnesses include Moses, Abraham, the apostle Paul, David, Isaiah, Joshua, Peter, James, John, the entire "Hall of Faith" as recorded in Hebrews 11, and, of course, Jesus Himself!

This incredible crowd is watching you. Their own accomplishments as well as their intimate awareness of your race are sure sources of momentum for you! Even if you stumble and fall, get up and keep moving, for this great throng is committed to your success in God!

The 20th Century New Testament says, "There is on every side of us, a great throng of witnesses."

William's translation says, "There's a vast crowd of spectators in the grandstands."

The Living Bible gives us an excellent picture: "Since we have such a huge crowd of men and women of faith watching us from the grandstands...let us run our race with patience."

Determine to Win

When the apostle Paul wrote the verse about "running the race," he used a sports example that the Hebrew people of his time could easily understand.

The illustration refers to the athletic games of ancient Greece, which were similar to our Olympics. When running a race, the athletes would be surrounded by huge crowds of enthusiastic people watching and cheering them on from the grandstands. It was just like the Olympic racing of today.

Paul wanted us to have this incredible picture fixed in our minds. He wanted us to determine to win our race!

Imagine those who have laid down their lives for the same cause for which you live. Imagine how Stephen, who was stoned to death for his commitment to Christ, is urging you ahead in your commitment. Imagine how Abraham, the father of our faith, would encourage you in your own walk. Imagine the best men and women God has ever produced giving you the "thumbs up" sign—boosting you forward to a faith that wins.

That means you are not alone in your struggles...or your gains. All that you do is important. Every godly choice and sacrifice you make now does make a difference—for all eternity! The great cloud around you knows you and is watching your race, and they await your victory!

Give them something to cheer about!

Endnote

1. *Dake's Annotated Reference Bible*, 79.

2. Dr. Kenneth Hagin, Sr. *Word of Faith Magazine* (June, 1991), 24(6):15.

Chapter 9

Babies, Children, and Heaven

Nothing quite touches us like the innocence and wonder of a little one. And nothing quite moves us like the death of a baby or child.

A fair and loving God has much to say about their place in Heaven.

Perhaps you have lost a child of your own, experienced a miscarriage, or the birth of a stillborn. You may be thinking of the loss of a baby belonging to a loved one or a friend. Others may recall a child who died of disease or a tragic accident, or by the hand of abortion.

God's promise is that the eternal purpose for these young lives will still be carried out. But first we must establish how the Scriptures view babies and children, and their awareness and accountability.

This is especially important when you consider how great a percentage of Heaven must involve these little ones. In our nation alone, 1.5 million babies are put in Heaven each and every year by abortion. This does not include the multiplied famines, disease, and abortions worldwide over thousands of years, which also took their toll of young lives.

From Conception

The world may be confused, but the Bible is very clear about when a person becomes a human being.

God Himself decided "when life begins." All throughout the Word of God, He makes it clear that from conception, there is a direct relationship with Him. According to Psalms, God knew you in your mother's womb while you were yet unformed substance, and He knew all the days He had planned for you while there had as yet been none of them (see Ps. 139:15-16).

The Gospel of Luke gives us other solid details:

And in the sixth month the angel Gabriel was sent from God unto a city of Galilee, named Nazareth.

To a virgin espoused to a man whose name was Joseph, of the house of David; and the virgin's name was Mary.

And the angel came in unto her, and said, Hail, thou that art highly favoured, the Lord is with thee: blessed art thou among women.

And when she saw him, she was troubled at his saying, and cast in her mind what manner of salutation this should be.

And the angel said unto her, Fear not, Mary: for thou hast found favour with God.

And, behold, ***thou shalt conceive in thy womb, and bring forth a son****, and shalt call His name JESUS.*

He shall be great, and shall be called the Son of the Highest: and the Lord God shall give unto Him the throne of His father David:

And He shall reign over the house of Jacob for ever; and of His kingdom there shall be no end.

Then said Mary unto the angel, How shall this be, seeing I know not a man?

And the angel answered and said unto her, The Holy Ghost shall come upon thee, and the power of the Highest shall overshadow thee: ***therefore also that holy thing which shall be born of thee shall be called the Son of God.***

And, behold, thy cousin Elisabeth, she hath also conceived a son in her old age: and this is the sixth month with her, who was called barren.

For with God nothing shall be impossible.

And Mary said, Behold the handmaid of the Lord; be it unto me according to thy word. And the angel departed from her.

And Mary arose in those days, and went into the hill country with haste, into a city of Juda;

And entered into the house of Zacharias, and saluted Elisabeth.

And it came to pass, that, ***when Elisabeth heard the salutation of Mary, the babe leaped in her womb;*** *and Elisabeth was filled with the Holy Ghost:*

And she spake out with a loud voice, and said, Blessed art thou among women, and blessed is the fruit of thy womb.

And whence is this to me, that the mother of my Lord should come to me?

For, lo, as soon as the voice of thy salutation sounded in mine ears, the babe leaped in my womb for joy.

And blessed is she that believed: for there shall be a performance of those things which were told her from the Lord.

Luke 1:26-45

Notice that God calls the baby in Elisabeth's womb "a child" at six months into her pregnancy. And, without the aid of any technology, He knew it was a boy! The child was still in Elisabeth's womb, yet God recognized his identity as a real human being. We know today that baby was John the Baptist.

These verses also tell us much about a child this young. This baby is so sensitive to spiritual things that when the anointing of God touched his mother, John jumped in her womb (verse 41). This baby was clearly not an undefined "blob of tissue," but a real human being!

We're also clearly told that Elisabeth conceived a "son" (verse 36), not an embryo or a zygote or a tissue. John was a son at *conception*!

Pastor Jack Hayford offers more insight from Luke in his book *I'll Hold You in Heaven.*[1]

And Mary abode with her about three months, and returned to her own house.

Luke 1:56

Hayford notes that when Mary conceived Jesus, she was told that Elisabeth was in her sixth month of pregnancy. Mary went to her cousin and spent the remaining three months of Elisabeth's pregnancy with her. That means that when Mary arrived, and Elisabeth was filled with the Holy Spirit and prophesied to her, the baby in Mary's womb could have only been a few days old.

Yet notice that the child in Mary's womb was spoken of as "alive" and as "the Lord" at that very moment. This baby, the Lord Himself, was no less a person for being only a young fetus; no less a person for being only a few days old (verses 42-43).

The angel, Gabriel, had already announced, "And, behold, thou shalt conceive in thy womb, and bring forth a son, and shalt call His name JESUS" (verse 31). Jesus was Jesus in the flesh at conception. He was the Lord from that moment forward.

Divine Destiny

The Bible never wavers about life beginning at conception. The first chapter of Jeremiah is more specific about our destiny from conception:

Then the word of the Lord came unto me, saying,

> *Before I formed thee in the belly* [womb] *I knew thee; and before thou camest forth out of the womb I sanctified thee, and I ordained thee a prophet unto the nations.*
>
> Jeremiah 1:4-5

Moffatt's translation of the Hebrew Old Testament says, "Before I formed you in the womb, I chose you." Knox's translation says, "Before I fashioned thee in thy mother's womb, I set you apart for Myself." The Amplified Bible says, "Before I formed you in the womb I knew and approved of you."

It is clear that God has a purpose for every child before he or she is ever born. God has intent and direction for that child from the moment of conception. That means God has a purpose for you too...for there are no exceptions!

Consider how intricate you were at only three months in the womb:

> "The third week, the lobes of the brain are distinguishable; the fourth week, the head and face are recognizable and the heart starts to beat; during weeks five and six, the eyes are identifiable and legs are putting on flesh and muscle; in the eighth week the embryo moves to the fetal stage and in the following weeks, sex can be identified; the baby can begin to turn its head, squint, frown, make a fist and even get the hiccups: all of this before the end of the first three months in the womb!"[2]

A God who creates this wonderfully has plans for every life.

No Mistakes

That is good news for each and every one of us, no matter what circumstances surrounded our birth. So you are not here as an accident or mistake. You are not here because a pill failed. You did not take God by surprise. He foreknew you before the womb!

God gave your life a divine purpose and destiny before you were ever conceived. Look at how David described our time in the womb:

> *My frame was not hidden from You when I was being formed in secret [and] intricately and curiously wrought [as if embroidered with various colors]...*
>
> *Your eyes saw my unformed substance, and in Your book all the days [of my life] were written before ever they took shape, when as yet there was none of them.*
>
> Psalm 139:15-16 AMP

The Bible in Basic English translates this same verse as, "Your eyes saw my unformed substance and in Your book all my days were recorded, even those which were purposed before they had come into being."

R.K. Harrison's translation of Hebrew into current English says of this same verse, "You perceived my shapeless substance and in your record were assessed the days that were intended for me before they ever existed."

With all assurance, you may surely say that you were planned and that your life has purpose! That is surely how God treats all His children.

An Eternal Blueprint

An even more intricate miracle is woven into Harrison's translation of verse 16. Notice it says that "In your *record* were assessed the days that were intended for me before they ever existed."

Jack Hayford also notes in *I'll Hold You in Heaven* that the "record" or "book" of which this verse speaks is the intricate "record" scientists know is a complete blueprint of your unique design and substance. It is you DNA cells!

God has so intimately planned each life that the whole "code" of people's future can be found in just one DNA cell. This is an amazing way to insure that even the tiniest infant who dies could be raised in Heaven.

Think of it. Microbiologists know that encoded into every cell of your body is the complete and unique plan of who you are. By looking at the DNA through a microscope, they can tell your sex, hair color, race, eyes, features, and to some degree, your approximate size.

Hayford states, "Every cell has the entire schematic of who you are. This means that even in the smallest collection of cells formulating the tissues of a miscarried or an aborted child, the encoded message of its physical development and appearance are already present."[3]

This means that God distinctly knows how a baby who has never been born would look at 12 years old...or 20...or "thirty something." As we've discovered, we are raised in Heaven to be our *idios* self, in glorified bodies that look like us (see 1 Cor. 15).

Most likely, all of us will appear as "thirty something," or our properly matured selves. It seems to also make sense this would be true of even the youngest baby, for the joys and depths of Heaven could best be grasped by a matured adult.

With this incredible blueprint of DNA, raising children to their *idios* self when they arrive in Heaven would easily be possible. It would not make a difference if that baby had never drawn a breath or if a young child had been destroyed in death. They will be raised up from death to look like themselves, without flaw, and it only takes one cell for God to do it. It is He who made and keeps the "record" of their life!

A Just God

How do we know that babies and children who die go to Heaven? The concept of accountability makes it clear.

We know that adults will be judged on their decision for Christ to determine whether or not they enter Heaven. God considers each person accountable for this decision. Yet a baby or young child is not able to make that choice.

Because the Scriptures are emphatic about God's fairness, to do anything other than accept children and babies into Heaven who die before the age of accountability would not be right.

Remember when Abraham and God met in Genesis? Abraham asked God if He would destroy the righteous along with the wicked in Sodom and Gomorrah (see Gen. 18). Abraham appealed to God's fairness. Of course, it was not God's desire to harm the righteous, and that is why He brought the issue before Abraham for intercession. He would not and did not destroy the righteous.

God will always do what is right—even to the point of coming down from Heaven to insure that a righteous lineage would begin, just as He did with Abraham and Sarah. That is also true with any human being who comes into God's presence. There could be no other just recourse than for any baby or child who died before becoming conscious of sin to go straight to Heaven. Jesus already paid the price for that child's salvation.

This would also include those who are mentally ill. A person may be 50 years old, but have the mind of a five-year-old. A just God could not hold such people accountable. They too would go straight to Heaven upon death.

That would also mean stillborn babies, miscarried babies, and newborns who die after a few days, as well as aborted babies and children who die before the age of accountability by tragedy, sickness, or accident, would go straight to Heaven.

This is in keeping with how God calls man to salvation.

For as in Adam all die, even so in Christ shall all be made alive.

1 Corinthians 15:22

It is important to understand that no one goes to hell because of Adam's sin. That would not be a fair act by a just God. If you go to hell, it will be because of your own sins. It will be because of the sins you have committed after the age of accountability, when you know you have done wrong and have sinned.

It is those sins that condemn a man to hell, unless he receives the forgiveness and cleansing blood of Christ; not sins that occur before a person is old enough to know that Jesus paid for them.

His Heavenly Provision

Not only does God provide for the entrance of babies and children into Heaven, He also tell us many things about His loving care for them.

The Bible clearly states that little ones mean much to God and that they have direct access to Him, whether they are alive on earth or in Heaven. Jesus Himself said:

> *Take heed that ye despise not one of these little ones; for I say unto you, That in heaven their angels do always behold the face of My Father which is in Heaven.*
>
> Matthew 18:10

There is direct access. Again, Jack Hayford notes in his book that the age that access is broken cannot be calendared. It varies from child to child. Still, one thing is clear: An unborn, stillborn, or other very young child who dies has not transgressed that union. There is a direct relationship with God that is open to them.

Angels

Through this same verse, we know that God indeed assigns angels to His children and babies. It is written that these angels communicate on their behalf to God.

Some people think that these same angels take on the responsibility of raising a child who dies prematurely. These angels, under God's supervision, would assist in that child's heavenly education.

It makes sense that our just and loving God is capable of making up any childhood lost here on earth. It also makes sense that He would personally step in to make up any lack! "Papa God" in His tender concern would make it right (see Rom. 8:15).

Think how much easier it would be for the child raised in God's presence...free from any of the earthly limitations, sin, and rebellion with which those on earth must contend!

Forgiveness

This chapter would not be complete without an understanding of the full plan of God as it concerns His little ones—even if their deaths were at our own hands. The frequency of abortion in this country has probably touched every reader of this book in some way.

God, however, had already seen our selfishness and sin, and in His plan for complete forgiveness, He made eternal provision to redeem us from it. Every person who is a believer in Christ and who has repented of his or her sin will have the privilege of seeing and knowing his or her lost children and embracing them in Heaven.

The scourge of condemnation is lifted forever through the blood of Jesus and the provision He made.

Consider King David and his infant son who died (see 2 Sam. 12:13-23). This little boy's death was the result of

David's sin. He had committed adultery with Bathsheba and then murdered her husband, Uriah, to cover up the sin. The prophet Nathan told David that the murder and the sin David committed would cost him his son's life.

The word of the Lord came to pass, and the little boy died after seven days. The death was David's fault. The situation is really not that much different from abortion.

Yet during the week between his son's birth and death, we see some amazing truths. Yes, there was a tragic consequence for David's sin. But there was also redemption.

We are told that during the seven days the little boy lived, David lay on his face praying and crying. He would not eat. He hardly slept; tears were his food. Finally, on the seventh day, the child died.

A Glad Reunion

Even in the most tragic of circumstances, we can be reconciled with our God through the shed blood of His Son and receive a glad reunion.

As Grant Jeffrey has so aptly said, "Where the Christian is concerned, death cannot defeat our love. It can only momentarily delay it. Heaven is the place where the joys of relationship are forever restored."[4]

King David was confident of this reunion. In light of eternity's length, even death is a minute delay. That means for every child lost, every miscarriage, every stillbirth, every accidental death of a child...and every abortion, those who hold fast in Christ are guaranteed a glad reunion.

What a great hope is extended to us by our heavenly Father. To those who have felt the emptiness when a child has gone on, God promises you as a believer that you will hold that child again.

He also assures you that your child has an eternal destiny and purpose that He Himself provides and continues. He promises you His own divine personal care of your loved one and the help of His angels. He promises you that great reunion day, a day of uninterrupted relationship. For though "they cannot come to you...you can go to them!"

These children of Heaven who have already joined that great cloud of witnesses themselves urge you onward!

Endnotes

1. Jack Hayford, *I'll Hold You in Heaven* (Ventura, CA: Regal Books, 1986).

2. *Life* Magazine reprint on the first trimester of life, copyright 1979.

3. Hayford, *I'll Hold You in Heaven*, 77.

4. Grant Jeffrey, *Heaven, the Last Frontier* (Toronto, Ontario: Frontier Research Publications, 1990), 188.

Chapter 10

The City of God

What joy we can discover about the actual place of Heaven we are headed to. We can know about the city of our God, our New Jerusalem! Look and see:

> *And I saw a new heaven and a new earth: for the first heaven and the first earth were passed away; and there was no more sea.*
>
> *And I John saw the holy city, new Jerusalem, coming down from God out of heaven, prepared as a bride adorned for her husband.*
>
> *And I heard a great voice out of heaven saying, Behold, the tabernacle of God is with men, and He will dwell with them, and they shall be His people, and God Himself shall be with them, and be their God.*
>
> *And God shall wipe away all tears from their eyes; and there shall be no more death, neither sorrow, nor crying, neither shall there be any more pain: for the former things are passed away.*

And He that sat upon the throne said, Behold, I make all things new. And He said unto me, Write: for these words are true and faithful.

And He said unto me, It is done. I am Alpha and Omega, the beginning and the end. I will give unto him that is athirst of the fountain of the water of life freely.

He that overcometh shall inherit all things; and I will be his God, and he shall be My son.

But the fearful, and unbelieving, and the abominable, and murderers, and whoremongers, and sorcerers, and idolaters, and all liars, shall have their part in the lake which burneth with fire and brimstone: which is the second death.

And there came unto me one of the seven angels which had the seven vials full of the seven last plagues, and talked with me, saying, Come hither, I will shew thee bride, the Lamb's wife.

And he carried me away in the spirit to a great and high mountain, and shewed me that great city, the holy Jerusalem, descending out of heaven from God,

Having the glory of God: and her light was like unto a stone most precious, even like a jasper stone, clear as crystal;

And had a wall great and high, and had twelve gates, and at the gates twelve angels, and names written thereon, which are the names of the twelve tribes of the children of Israel:

On the east three gates; on the north three gates; on the south three gates; and on the west three gates.

And the wall of the city had twelve foundations, and in them the names of the twelve apostles of the Lamb.

And he that talked with me had a golden reed to measure the city, and the gates thereof, and the wall thereof.

And the city lieth foursquare, and the length is as large as the breadth: and he measured the city with the reed, twelve thousand furlongs. The length and the breadth and the height of it are equal.

And he measured the wall thereof, an hundred and forty and four cubits, according to the measure of a man, that is, of the angel.

And the building of the wall of it was of jasper: and the city was pure gold, like unto clear glass.

And the foundations of the wall of the city were garnished with all manner of precious stones. The first foundation was jasper; the second, sapphire; the third, a chalcedony; the fourth, an emerald;

The fifth, sardonyx; the sixth, sardius; the seventh, chrysolyte; the eighth, beryl; the ninth, a topaz; the tenth, a chrysoprasus; the eleventh, a jacinth; the twelfth, an amethyst.

And the twelve gates were twelve pearls: every several gate was of one pearl: and the street of the city was pure gold, as it were transparent glass.

And I saw no temple therein: for the Lord God Almighty and the Lamb are the temple of it.

And the city had no need of the sun, neither of the moon, to shine in it: for the glory of God did lighten it, and the Lamb is the light thereof.

And the nations of them which are saved shall walk in the light of it: and the kings of the earth do bring their glory and honour into it.

And the gates of it shall not be shut at all by day: for there shall be no night there.

And they shall bring the glory and honour of the nations into it.

And there shall in no wise enter into it any thing that defileth, neither whatsoever worketh abomination, or maketh a lie: but they which are written in the Lamb's book of life.

And he shewed me a pure river of water of life, clear as crystal, proceeding out of the throne of God and of the Lamb.

In the midst of the street of it, and on either side of the river, was there the tree of life, which bare twelve manner of fruits, and yielded her fruit every month: and the leaves of the tree were for the healing of the nations.

And there shall be no more curse: but the throne of God and of the Lamb shall be in it; and His servants shall serve Him:

> *And they shall see His face; and His name shall be in their foreheads.*
>
> *And there shall be no night there; and they need no candle, neither light of the sun; for the Lord God giveth them light: and they shall reign for ever and ever.*
>
> Revelation 21:1–22:5

This description of Heaven may seem beyond our imaginations! Yet as we look further into these verses, we'll find that its magnificence is truly real.

Many people think these descriptions of our eternal city are pleasant allegories. What a tragic loss that is to our hope of what is to come! The same God who created man from the dust of the earth has no problem making good on His word of the riches He has used in building the New Jerusalem.

"...Eye hath not seen, nor ear heard" of the full creation that awaits us (1 Cor. 2:9). The paltry riches of this earth could only be considered the most minute reflection of the place for God's own throne!

God has already given us great insight as to where this city will be and what it will be like.

Renewed Earth

The New Jerusalem is presently being built by God in Heaven. It is His city, and it comprises the fullness of Heaven now.

Yet the Scriptures tell us that after the 1,000-year millennial reign of Jesus, God is going to make a *new heaven* and a *new earth.* Then the entire New Jerusalem shall descend to take its place forever on this remade earth:

> *And I saw a new heaven and a new earth: for the first heaven and the first earth were passed away; and there was no more sea.*
>
> Revelation 21:1

The word *new* in this text does not mean something that is brand-new. It is not something that never existed and is now being made. Rather this Greek word is *kainos*, which means "qualitatively new"; to "renew"; a "renewing."

This old earth will be far different when God is through with it. We haven't seen anything yet!

God will fully renew the earth of which He originally created and said, "It is good!" It will be as He first intended. He will make the atmosphere or sky and all that we know new.

The Greek word for "earth" in this context means "soil," or "ground." As God renews the earth's soils, all the pollutants and ravages of man's sin, rebellion, and misuse will be burned up—and the earth and sky will become perfectly pure and clean again. He tells us how:

> *But the day of the Lord will come as a thief in the night; in the which the heavens shall pass away with a great noise, and the elements shall melt with fervent heat, the earth also and the works that are therein shall be burned up.*
>
> 2 Peter 3:10

Plausible Science

Many people believe that this kind of a melting, burning, and renewing of the earth will be some sort of a hydrogen explosion. For example, in the 1980's the Air Force detonated a hydrogen bomb in the Bikini Atolls, a part of the Marshall Islands. The explosion was so violent that it sparked a chain reaction of three more explosions in the atmosphere.

The ripping of these neutrons, electrons, and protons was so intense that the water around the island actually caught fire. Scientists know that had a fourth explosion occurred, it would have begun a chain reaction of explosions around the world. These explosions would have destroyed the earth's atmosphere, as well as burn its soil and the ocean.

It is very plausible that in God's time, He could use such an explosion to melt the elements and begin the transformation of the earth. Although we may not know exactly how such a renewal will happen, one thing is sure: It will happen! There will be a "new" earth.

New Earth's Terrain

As the atmosphere and the earth are renewed, we know from Scripture there will be "no more sea." (Rev. 21:1). This does not mean there won't be any water in the new earth, for many Scriptures tell us there will be rivers and small seas (see Ps. 72:7-8; Is. 42:4,10; Jer. 5:22; 33:22; Rev. 22:1-2). Nevertheless, the major oceans would be done away with in the new earth, which means that millions of additional square miles of land would become inhabitable.

These new pristine lands are the perfect place for the King of kings to live forever with His people. As this habitable land mass multiplies, it could easily fit the New Jerusalem as it descends from Heaven. What a city it will be!

And I John saw the holy city, new Jerusalem, coming down from God out of heaven, prepared as a bride adorned for her husband.

And I heard a great voice out of heaven saying, Behold, the tabernacle of God is with men, and He will dwell with them, and they shall be His people, and God Himself shall be with them, and be their God.

Revelation 21:2-3

And I saw no temple therein: for the Lord God Almighty and the Lamb are the temple of it.

Revelation 21:22

That means the Lord God Almighty Himself, and the Lamb, Jesus, will have Their thrones among us in this holy city, Their permanent residence upon the renewed earth. They have chosen to dwell with us forever, not some place billions of miles away. What an eternal privilege and delight:

And there shall be no more curse: but the throne of God and of the Lamb shall be in it; and His servants shall serve Him:

And they shall see His face; and His name shall be in their foreheads.

And there shall be no night there; and they need no candle, neither light of the sun; for the Lord God giveth them light: and they shall reign for ever and ever.

Revelation 22:3-5

His City

We can find at least nine descriptions to help us better know the city of our God.

1. It's the *holy city* (Rev. 21:2).
2. It's the *Bride of the Lamb*, the place of His people's dwelling who have been prepared to be united with His Son (Rev. 21:2).
3. It's the *Tabernacle of God*, where His throne abides (Rev. 21:3; 13:6; 15:5).
4. It's the *holy Jerusalem.* It's the holy place where God Himself dwells (Rev. 21:10).
5. It's the *great city*, the capital of the universe and matchless in splendor (Rev. 21:10).
6. It's the *new Jerusalem* (Rev. 21:2).
7. It's the *heavenly Jerusalem*, for it far surpasses the earthly Jerusalem often idolized by men on earth (Heb. 12:22-23).
8. It's *"My Father's house."* Jesus spoke of this city when He said He would go to prepare a place for us. It is indeed a place of many mansions. "If it were not so, I would have told you" (see Jn. 14:1-3).
9. It's the *city of the Living God* (Heb. 12:22-23).

And the beauty of the place?

At best, it would be difficult to communicate the magnitude of this city's beauty. It is a city whose builder and maker is God! (See Hebrews 11:10.)

Our matchless Architect and His work are far beyond our comprehension. Nothing could be more spectacular or enthralling. If you were to take all the great cities of our world, such as Paris, London, New York, or Los Angeles, they would be like "ghettos" in comparison to our Father's house.

The most spectacular accomplishment of man—the most grand architecture, the most significant skyscraper or valiant cathedral—are all still limited, since they are creations of the hand of man.

Even the most beautiful natural scene you could imagine will pale in comparison to the colors, magnificence, and panoramic grandeur of this City of God made by the Creator Himself.

Just one glimpse of this city from John in Revelation is enough to take your breath away. God has given the creation of this city His most glorious effort—and anything to which we could compare it will fade miserably in its light.

We can only contemplate with awe what we do not know!

Dimensions

Consider just the size of this city.

The passage in Revelation written by John describes the city's dimensions as a square, 12,000 furlongs by 12,000 furlongs (see Rev. 21:10-21). Twelve thousand furlongs is 1500 miles! That means this city is 1500 miles long and 1500 miles wide. That is 2,250,000 square miles!

To envision its size, imagine the distance from the Rocky Mountains to the Appalachian Mountains, and then from the

Canadian border to the Gulf of Mexico. That is an approximate 1500-mile square.

If you were to form a square of land from Dallas, Texas, to Washington, D.C., and back, you'd also have an example of the size of the New Jerusalem. That is about 625 million city blocks as we know them!

There's more. The city is also 1500 miles high. Our atmosphere as we know it now is only about 15 or 20 miles high. God has already promised that He will remake the atmosphere in our recreated earth. He would have to remake it just to accommodate His city!

For years, people have puzzled over how this city could be that high. Many artists have rendered strange drawings of New Jerusalem stacked on top of itself like high-rise apartments.

A closer look at the Scriptures reveals that New Jerusalem is not just some type of tall cube. Its description tells us that it has an enormous wall around the city. You would not need a wall if the city were cubed! The sides of the cube itself would be the walls.

It would be more credible if the city were actually a series of mountains. These mountains would begin inside the walls as low foothills, and then increase in height until the highest peak or mountain range is 1500 miles high. This peak would be Mount Zion itself.[1] Considering the city in this fashion clears up many misconceptions and allows us to better visualize the actual New Jerusalem.

Further biblical references support this mountain concept:

> *But ye are come unto* **mount** *Sion, and unto the city of the living God, the heavenly Jerusalem, and to an innumerable company of angels.*
>
> Hebrews 12:22

J.B. Rotherham's translation of this same verse says, "But you have approached Zion's mountain." It is clearly called a mountain, and is pictured this way throughout the Bible.

A look at Mount Zion in Israel today gives us an earthly example. It is a small model of the heavenly Jerusalem that will sit on Heaven's Mount Zion.

Other verses in the Book of Revelation also lend credence to this notion. John writes, "And I looked, and, lo, a Lamb stood on the mount Sion, and with Him an hundred forty and four thousand, having His Father's name written in their foreheads" (Rev. 14:1). John thus saw Jesus on Mount Zion in the New Jerusalem.

What a day it shall be when we see that city crowned with the splendor of Mount Zion, which the Psalms call "the perfection of beauty" (Ps. 50:2).

A Place for All

On this highest mountain is where we would find the throne room of God Himself. From this apex, God reigns over the entire universe.

Moses used this same pattern to build the earthly tabernacle, in which Israel worshiped God (see Heb. 8:5). Yet the heavenly temple far exceeds anything we have ever known on earth, for "Christ is not entered into the holy places made with hands" (Heb. 9:24a). In fact, John saw Jesus Himself appear as the tabernacle of God, far surpassing the glory or need for any building (see Rev. 21:3).

Although we are not told the exact size of Mount Zion in the New Jerusalem, it must be huge. The floor of the throne room itself is described like a sea of glass, clear as crystal (see Rev. 4:6). It also must be large enough for an untold number of glorified believers who will stand before God's throne (see Rev. 7:9), as well as 144,000 who will stand with Jesus (see Rev. 14:3). Surely there will be innumerable angels as well!

On this highest peak, the home of God Himself, are banquet facilities immense enough to hold every believer or saint who ever lived (see Rev. 19:9). Our first gathering, the marriage supper of the Lamb, may be the first of perhaps millions of such gatherings throughout eternity.

Surrounding Mount Zion for hundreds of miles would be mountains and valleys on which are built the "many mansions" of the saints. The Greek word for "mansion" is *mone*, meaning "residence" (see Jn. 14:2). That means that from the home of God, you can see the residences of His people for as far as the eye can see.

You have a residence there! Jesus is preparing a place for every Christian. We know that the places God is building for His children must be very special. Imagine living in God's own neighborhood!

The Father's house itself must be beyond description. However, nothing we could imagine about these creations could hold a candle to the glorious presence of God Himself. His magnificence will far outshine any other aspect of Heaven.

Streets of Gold

Let's picture the City of God itself.

There is a great river that flows out from the throne of God (see Rev. 22:1). This mighty river flows down from the top of Mount Zion just as rivers flow from mountains on earth. As this great river builds and tumbles and cascades down the majestic mountain to the base, it forms 12 beautiful rivers that flow throughout the New Jerusalem.

Each river flows toward one of the 12 different gates of the square City, which would place three on each side. From these gates extend 12 streets or boulevards (see Rev. 22:2; 21:21). This is not to say there are no other streets. It could just mean there is easy access to the New Jerusalem and that travel is a part of life in the city.

Yet consider the path for our travel! We are told that the streets are made of pure gold. Gold without impurities is transparent—you can see through it. Imagine a street of gold lined by a crystal clear river that bubbles with the life of God Himself (see Rev. 22:1-2). Consider that the beauty of each of these boulevards and rivers extends for 1500 miles across the entire New Jerusalem! Such will be our portion in the eternal city.

His Glory

What a wonder this New Jerusalem will be! Yet crowning the splendor will be God's own glory.

From Mount Zion, 1500 miles high, God's glory will surely shine so brightly that it will light up all of New Jerusalem.

The Scriptures say that His glory will *perilampo* or "shine round about" for 1500 miles in every direction. Though the sun and moon are still in existence, this city will have no need of their light (see Rev. 21:23).

Can you imagine His brilliance shining off of shimmering pure crystal rivers, rebounding off streets of gold, walls of jasper, gates of pearl, and foundation walls garnished with the colors of the rainbow?

Surely it is beyond our understanding. But it is not a dream. It is not a fairy tale or a fantasy...rather, it is our real, eternal home! It is our Father's house!

No mountain range of the Grand Tetons can compare. No sunset or postcard of the most beautiful paradise can rival it. No Sistine Chapel or Empire State Building can come close to it. Nothing can compare with the scenes from the mountains of Heaven that will landscape the New Jerusalem. The pristine grandeur of this place will be made new every day by the presence of God Himself.

The resplendent views will quench every thirst we can ever have for freshness and beauty. No doubt, we will stand in stunned silence as we first behold the magnitude of God's handiwork in our heavenly home. Then we shall behold the face of the Architect Himself!

Together, we'll praise our Father for His lovingkindness, and look to the mountain of the Lamb with thanksgiving.

Our hearts will cry with thanks forever as we consider a life so abundant and eternal. We too shall join the host of Heaven as we shout:

> *Great is the Lord, and greatly to be praised in the city of our God, in the mountain of His holiness.*
>
> *Beautiful for situation, the joy of the whole earth, is mount Zion, on the sides of the north, the city of the great King.*
>
> Psalm 48:1-2

Endnote

1. Finis Jennings Dake, *God's Plan for Man* (Lawrenceville, GA: Dake Bible Sales, Inc., 1949, 1977), 990.

Chapter 11

More of the New Jerusalem

For too long, we have pictured the pearly gates of Heaven with Saint Peter checking I.D.'s. We've seen some loosely structured cloud with a registration desk. But there's quite a bit more we can know about the majestic entrance to our New Jerusalem!

> *And had a wall great and high, and had twelve gates, and at the gates twelve angels, and names written thereon, which are the names of the twelve tribes of the children of Israel:*
>
> *On the east three gates; on the north three gates; on the south three gates; and on the west three gates.*
>
> *And the wall of the city had twelve foundations, and in them the names of the twelve apostles of the Lamb.*
>
> Revelation 21:12-14

There are 12 gates or entrances to the New Jerusalem. Upon each gate is engraved the name of one of the 12 tribes of Israel: Reuben, Simeon, Judah, Issachar, Zebulun, Ephraim, Manasseh, Benjamin, Dan, Asher, Gad, and Naphtali (see Gen 49:1-27).

There are three gates on each side of the square wall surrounding the city. This means there are three gates to the north, three to the south, three to the east, and three to the west. On a "square" compass, this represents a gate for all possible directions: North, northeast, northwest; South, southeast, southwest; East, eastnorth, eastsouth; and West, westnorth, westsouth.

This is God's literal representation that Heaven is accessible for every man from every place. In other words, you "can get there from here"! God has extended His welcome in all directions to every man.

Yet the composition of His gates describes the price to enter such glory:

> *And the twelve gates were twelve pearls; every several gate was of one pearl: and the street of the city was pure gold, as it were transparent glass.*
>
> Revelation 21:21

It says that each gate is made out of one huge pearl. When we think of the "pearly gates," it is doubtful that many people grasp their full significance.

Gates of Pearl

The pearl gates represent Jesus Christ, the Lamb slain for our sins. They speak of God's salvation and of the precious redemption of His people.

The choice of the pearl can be understood from the Gospel of Matthew, in which Jesus said:

> *Again, the kingdom of heaven is like unto a merchant man, seeking goodly pearls:*

Who, when he had found one pearl of great price, went and sold all that he had, and bought it.

Matthew 13:45-46

Simply stated, Jesus Himself is the pearl of great price! When we sell out to Him, we gain His salvation. Not even our lives are worth the price of that gift!

There may be other "pearls" in this life that seem great. There are pearls of pleasure, pearls of learning, and pearls of material wealth. But Jesus is truly a pearl like no other. All that you could give for Him is a small price to pay!

Jesus is the entrance to true wealth. He is the only entrance to abundant life now and eternal life later with all its riches. He is the only remedy for sin and separation from God. Jesus said, "I am the way, the truth, and the life: no man cometh unto the Father, but by Me" (Jn. 14:6).

Jesus paid with His own blood on the cross that you might have access to that pearl. Just as a pearl is obtained through the suffering of the host, so Jesus died that you might have the true riches and entrance into the glorious City of God.

Can you imagine the beauty of a pearl large enough to allow passage through it into Heaven? Can you imagine the incomparable and unique beauty with which each gate must shine? All who enter this great city must enter through the gates of pearl—through Jesus. There is no other way.

Also, the gates to that city are never closed (see Rev. 21:25). God loves these gates. They represent to Him the love He has for you, the salvation He offers to every man, and the price He paid with His own Son:

The Lord loveth the gates of Zion more than all the dwellings of Jacob.

Psalm 87:2

Tears for Pearl

The gates of pearl have another key significance.

A pearl often represents tears. When a tiny grain of sand gets inside an oyster, the oyster secretes a fluid to protect itself. These "tears" or secretions inside the oyster are actually what forms the pearl.

Jesus, the pearl of great price, also wept. Sin and death and its great and painful irritation caused Him to weep. Pearls represent these tears.

This means that as you enter through these gates, you have passed through your last tear. Jesus paid the price. If you have suffered seasons of weeping, great hope lies ahead. If tears have been your food, and grief has caused your eyes to burn with irritation, you will never experience that pain again. Anguish will no longer find you as you pass through the gates of pearl:

And God shall wipe away all tears from their eyes; and there shall be no more death, neither sorrow, nor crying, neither shall there be any more pain....

Revelation 21:4

Know today with confidence your glad entrance to this Kingdom. Know surely that earth has no sorrows that Heaven cannot heal!

Foundation Stones

If the gateway into the city of Heaven is not enough to stop us in awe of its splendor, consider the wall to which these gates are attached!

And the wall of the city had twelve foundations, and in them the names of the twelve apostles of the Lamb.

And he that talked with me had a golden reed to measure the city, and the gates thereof, and the wall thereof.

And the city lieth foursquare, and the length is as large as the breadth: and he measured the city with the reed, twelve thousand furlongs. The length and the breadth and height of it are equal.

And he measured the wall thereof, an hundred and forty and four cubits, according to the measure of a man, that is, of the angel.

And the building of the wall of it was of jasper: and the city was pure gold, like unto clear glass.

And the foundations of the wall of the city were garnished with all manner of precious stones. The first foundation was jasper; the second, sapphire; the third, a chalcedony; the fourth, an emerald;

The fifth, sardonyx; the sixth, sardius; the seventh, chrysolyte; the eighth, beryl; the ninth, a topaz; the tenth, a chrysoprasus; the eleventh, a jacinth; the twelfth, an amethyst.

Revelation 21:14-20

We've already seen that the base of this city is 1500 miles long and 1500 miles wide. There is also a wall around this entire square; and according to the Scriptures, it is 240 feet high (verse 17). That is 24 stories high!

This wall sits on a foundation that is in itself spectacular. It is made from stones of jasper, sapphire, chalcedony, emerald, sardonyx, sardius, chrysolyte, beryl, topaz, chrysoprasus, jacinth, and amethyst (see Rev. 21:19-20).

Most likely these massive precious stones are not stacked on top of each other with the wall on top. Rather, they are probably laid end to end to form the foundation for the wall itself.

Clarke's Commentary calls these foundation stones "thresholds" for the gates of pearl, of which, as you'll remember, there are three on each side of the square.

Since each side of the wall is 1500 miles long and has three gates, that means each gate would be about 500 miles apart if the length was proportionally divided. That would mean these incredible 12 foundation stones each run for 500 miles underneath each gate!

Can you imagine a 500-mile long emerald? Then under the next gate, a topaz of similar length?

Unlike our foundations today, these stones are probably above ground and very visible. Experts say that a foundation is usually at least one-fifth of a wall's height. That means each of these foundation stones is also 48 feet tall. Can you imagine an emerald that is 48 feet tall by 500 miles long, into which is centered a huge gate of pearl?

Only God could prepare such a place! Such a miraculous city!

Out of His great love and covenant faithfulness, God has written upon each of these 12 foundation stones the name of one of Christ's disciples: Matthew, Mark, Luke, John.... He has given these "regular" men who followed in faith a place in the extraordinary—to be celebrated forever.

John Gilmore, in *Probing Heaven*, states that these foundation stones represent God's unfolding revelation through the apostles, which continues to form the basis for Christian hope hereafter.[1] God has already made the very foundation for our future hope the foundation walls of His city!

The Magnificent Wall

On top of these breathtaking foundation stones lies the wall itself. It is made of jasper, and is also 240 feet high (see Rev. 21:17-18).

The Greek word for "jasper" is *yashpheh*, which means "the colors of fire."[2]

Think of the last time you looked into a fireplace and gazed at the dancing colors of fire. Recall the warmth, peace, and comfort you felt as you beheld its beauty. Now amplify this beyond a height you can imagine, and you will see the wall of New Jerusalem that sits on top of the precious foundation stones of many colors. Don't forget the gates of pearl!

Add to that the brilliance of the glory of God Himself shining through and around these precious gems! We shall behold it and see!

Forever New

Thank God that on the day we enter that city, we shall be our glorified selves. It is doubtful our present flesh could withstand such indescribable glory! Yet as our "proper selves," whom He created us to be for eternity, we shall drink it in with joy!

If that is not enough, consider that what we behold will never grow old. Everything in this city will be rejuvenated daily by the presence of the living God. Many things we enjoy in this life fade as we see them again—not so in Heaven. God's splendor and glory will make it all new every morning!

The City Inside

As we enter the city and venture beyond the matchless gates and walls, there is yet more wonder to behold:

> *And he shewed me a pure river of water of life, clear as crystal, proceeding out of the throne of God and of the Lamb.*
>
> *In the midst of the street of it, and on either side of the river, was there the tree of life, which bare twelve manner of fruits, and yielded her fruit every month: and the leaves of the tree were for the healing of the nations.*
>
> Revelation 22:1-2

Beside the flowing rivers and great boulevards of God, there are "trees of life." These fruit trees are different from what we know today—these bear fruit every month.

Don't just picture a few trees; we will most likely see orchards that extend 1500 miles in every direction!

Have you ever been in an apple orchard when it is in full bloom, or an orange grove at the peak of its fragrance? Have you seen the cherry blossoms in their fullness and glory? Imagine the aroma filling the air in New Jerusalem. It will not be a short season of fragrance, but an aroma of a multitude of heavenly fruit trees that bud, bloom, and produce fruit every month!

You are invited to this place, forever. The crisp, clear mountain breezes will gently wind their way through the valleys of New Jerusalem and carry the fragrance of these orchards to fill the entire new earth. Such wonder awaits us!

Consider your hope today:

> There's no disappointment in heaven;
> No weariness, sorrow, or pain:
> No hearts that are bleeding and broken.
> No song with a minor refrain.
> The clouds of our earthly horizon
> Will never appear in the sky,
> For all will be sunshine and gladness,
> With never a sob nor a sigh.
>
> We'll never pay rent on our mansion,
> The taxes will never come due:
> Our garments will never grow threadbare,
> But always be fadeless and new.
> We'll never be hungry or thirsty,
> Nor languish in poverty there,

For all the rich bounties of heaven
His sanctified children will share.

There'll never be crepe on the door-knob,
No funeral train in the sky:
No graves on the hillsides of glory,
For there we shall never more die.
The old will be young there forever,
Transformed in a moment of time;
Immortal we'll stand in his likeness,
The stars and the sun to outshine.

I'm bound for that beautiful city
My Lord has prepared for His own
Where all the redeemed of all ages
Sing "Glory" around the white throne;
Sometimes I grow homesick for heaven,
And the glories I there shall behold:
What a joy that will be when my Savior I see,
In that beautiful city gold.

F.M. Lehman

Endnotes

1. John Gilmore, *Probing Heaven* (Grand Rapids, MI: Baker Book House, 1989), 117.

2. *Vine's Expository Dictionary of Biblical Words* (Westwood, NJ: Barbour and Company, Inc.; 1940 publication by Oliphants L.T.D.).

Chapter 12

The Final Ages Begin

The day is surely coming when the New Jerusalem will descend to this planet, and believers in Christ will live in that city with God.

When shall these things be? Will there be anyone else to share the renewed earth with us? What will be the future of man?

The devil did not destroy God's ultimate plan for man and the earth. Satan's destruction and havoc only temporarily delayed it. That means the best is yet to come! God's plan is sure.

The devil will be destroyed, and man will become all that God has designed for him from the very beginning of time. To truly grasp the promise of Heaven and the reality of an eternity planned by the Lord, let's look at God's order of things for the end of the ages.

As the ages draw to a close, God in His mercy again gives gracious opportunities for mankind to choose His Kingdom. Of course, not all people will make that choice, and we'll see the tragic penalties that follow.

We'll begin with Revelation chapter 20. This is just after the tribulation period and at the very beginning of the thousand years where Jesus Christ will rule the earth, called the "millennial reign."

Most scriptural interpretations believe the Church, or people of God, will be "raptured" or caught away with Christ before the seven years of tribulation begin. That means born-again believers will already be in God's presence—spared the torments of that terrible time.

Though some may debate if the Church is caught away before the tribulation, during the tribulation, or after the tribulation, we can all agree that the Bible is clear that at whatever time it happens, we will be caught up into Heaven "in the twinkling of an eye" before the millennial reign of Jesus begins.

The Tribulation

According to the Book of Revelation, the tribulation period will be seven years upon the earth. There will be three and one-half good years, and three and one-half bad years.

During those seven years, the antichrist will be revealed and start his reign of terror on the earth. In his misread charisma, he will lead many to destruction as the full instrument of the devil himself. It is a devastating period when millions will die because of his deceit and their own willfulness.

The following order of these end-time events are taken from the text of the Revelation Seminars conducted by Hilton Sutton, a respected Bible scholar.

First, lucifer will reveal his true vile character during these years, and the full extent of his wicked, murderous nature. One-quarter of the world's population will die as a result of the four horsemen of the Apocalypse. One-third of those remaining will then be slaughtered by a 200 million-man Oriental army.

The Bible tells us that between the horsemen, the plagues, the vast armies, and the final battle of Armageddon, nearly one-half of the world's population will be destroyed. Two billion people will die in seven years' time! It's little wonder we are told that the blood will run like rivers up to the horses' bridles (see Rev. 14:20).

The Necessity of Choice

No person wants to face the antichrist. This being is the most vicious and hate-filled person to ever exist. The death and destruction accomplished at his hand will be fueled by the fires of hell and satan himself.

Yet many today still put off their decision for Christ. They pacify their slumbering souls by thinking these things will never happen. Some people believe this account to be a fanciful religious fairy tale to scare people to the Lord.

Yet the same God who promises the reality of Heaven also promises the reality of hell and destruction. The same God who has kept a million promises declares this will happen.

God's longsuffering is the only delay you will see—so that as many people as possible may come to Christ and be saved. Without Jesus, no matter how well you have lived, your future holds the gaping jaws of hell.

The tribulation period on earth is only a sample of what hell will be like for all eternity. It's a time you will want to be "hid in Christ."

Satan Bound

As the tribulation draws to a close, one-half of the world's population will have been destroyed. Another half will remain. At this time, satan will be bound for a thousand years:

> *And I saw an angel come down from heaven, having the key of the bottomless pit and a great chain in his hand.*
>
> *And he laid hold on the dragon, that old serpent, which is the Devil, and Satan, and bound him a thousand years,*
>
> *And cast him into the bottomless pit, and shut him up, and set a seal upon him, that he should deceive the nations no more, till the thousand years should be fulfilled: and after that he must be loosed a little season.*
>
> Revelation 20:1-3

A strong angel, most likely Michael, God's war angel, will come down and confine lucifer in chains. Satan will be held in hell for the entire millennium, and Jesus will begin His 1,000-year reign.

During this reign, natural men who are left on earth will not have to face the devil. The nations and the peoples who survive the tribulation will be ruled by Jesus Himself.

However, these people will have no other choice than to submit to the Lord. The whole earth will be under Christ's

Kingdom. Without lucifer's deceit and distractions, this will be a far easier alternative! Man's eyes will be unobstructed to see the goodness of God.

During Christ's reign, those who have been raised in the rapture with Him will also help Him reign over these peoples on the earth:

> *And I saw thrones, and they sat upon them, and judgment was given unto them: and I saw the souls of them that were beheaded for the witness of Jesus, and for the word of God, and which had not worshipped the beast, neither his image, neither had received his mark upon their foreheads, or in their hands; and they lived and reigned with Christ a thousand years.*
>
> *But the rest of the dead lived not again until the thousand years were finished. This is the first resurrection.*
>
> *Blessed and holy is he that hath part in the first resurrection: on such the second death hath no power, but they shall be priests of God and of Christ, and shall reign with Him a thousand years.*
>
> Revelation 20:4-6

This first resurrection is referring to the rapture of the Church, when "the dead in Christ shall rise first" and we "which are alive and remain shall be caught up together with them in the clouds to meet the Lord..." (1 Thess. 4:16-17).

The Greek word for "throne" is *thronos*, meaning "stately seats of authority." God has promised that His own people, made righteous and given eternal life by His hand, shall also rule and reign! For 1,000 years, those of us who had part in the first resurrection shall be rulers and priests of God under Jesus Christ.

Together with Him, we will command the nations of the world. There will be no other governments, as in the past, which man made to rule or give order to the earth. There will be no trade unions, political parties, or any other form of man-made regimes. The people of God will be in charge of managing the Kingdom of God on this earth.

We will see the world operate according to the law of the Lord as we fill governing positions all over this planet. Without the influence of satan, there will be no crime or drug abuse, no violence in the streets, or any of the other horrors of a society that has exchanged His standards for their own.

Once again, in the kindness of a heavenly Father who loves us, God gives time for those who remain to see the righteousness of God and choose His Kingdom. Truly, He is not willing that "any should perish, but that all should come to repentance" (2 Pet. 3:9).

What a revelation it will be for those with eyes to see. The Bible tells us that even the animal kingdom will be at peace. The lion and the lamb will lie down together. The wolf and the calf will eat together. The children will play in safety without fear of man or beast. Even an asp will not harm them. This will be a glorious thousand years!

> *The wolf also shall dwell with the lamb, and the leopard shall lie down with the kid; and the calf and the young lion and the fatling together; and a little child shall lead them.*

And the cow and the bear shall feed; their young ones shall lie down together: and the lion shall eat straw like the ox.

And the sucking child shall play on the hole of the asp, and the weaned child shall put his hand on the cockatrice' den.

They shall not hurt nor destroy in all My holy mountain: for the earth shall be full of the knowledge of the Lord, as the waters cover the sea.

Isaiah 11:6-9

Still, all men shall not be satisfied.

Satan Loosed

At the end of Christ's millennial reign, satan will again be loosed for a season—his final "hurrah."

And when the thousand years are expired, Satan shall be loosed out of his prison,

And shall go out to deceive the nations which are in the four quarters of the earth, Gog and Magog, to gather them together to battle: the number of whom is as the sand of the sea.

And they went up on the breadth of the earth, and compassed the camp of the saints about, and the beloved city: and fire came down from God out of heaven, and devoured them.

Revelation 20:7-9

Once again, the devil himself will attempt to deceive the nations. He will be successful to a small degree. During the millennial reign of Jesus, all men were compelled to obey Him. Yet when given a choice, many people will still not want to serve the Lord.

According to the lust, greed, and evil nature that is in man without Christ, they still desire to rule themselves. They will have one final opportunity. Lucifer will lead these rebels in a final war against Jerusalem. He will gather an army that is as vast as the sand of the sea in number.

That battle will be the last on earth as we now know it. It won't be much of a war, however; God has already made this final victory plain and simple. The Bible barely mentions the struggle...except to say that God wins as fire comes down out of Heaven and devours all these adversaries (see Rev. 20:9).

Surely that is no surprise!

The White Throne Judgment

This final battle is the last event on earth as we know it. The unrighteous nations are devoured, and the saved nations remain. The nations of those who stand with Christ are not destroyed.

At this time, every person who has ever lived and refused to align himself with Christ will stand before God at the great white throne judgment. Satan too will receive his final sentence:

> *And the devil that deceived them was cast into the lake of fire and brimstone, where the beast and the false prophet are, and shall be tormented day and night for ever and ever.*

And I saw a great white throne, and Him that sat on it, from whose face the earth and the heaven fled away; and there was found no place for them.

And I saw the dead, small and great, stand before God; and the books were opened: and another book was opened, which is the book of life: and the dead were judged out of those things which were written in the books, according to their works.

And the sea gave up the dead which were in it; and death and hell delivered up the dead which were in them: and they were judged every man according to their works.

And death and hell were cast into the lake of fire. This is the second death.

And whosoever was not found written in the book of life was cast into the lake of fire.

Revelation 20:10-15

The devil is thus completely defeated and bound to hell with no reprieve, to be tormented forever.

All the rest who have rejected God—people from the beginning of time—also receive their sentence for eternity. They include those people who did not accept Jesus through the ages, those who took the "mark of the beast" (satan's mark) during the tribulation period, and the people who were part of the unrighteous nations who rebelled against Christ at the end of the millennium. All these people will be thrown into hell, the eternal lake of fire.

The Church in Heaven is not part of this judgment. Glorified saints were already judged 1,000 years earlier. Even then, our judgment did not concern entrance to Heaven but rather the reward we will receive for our obedience to God.

Likewise, the natural people who make up the saved nations that stood with Christ during the millennium are not judged. They are in Heaven, but they do not have glorified bodies. Why? They were not a part of the first resurrection.

These people too would not have to stand before the white throne. They have already chosen the Lord.

The Earth Remade

It is during this time of judgment that we find all peoples taken up to Heaven, whether for judgment and hell or for eternal life.

> *And I saw a great white throne, and Him that sat on it, from whose face the earth and the heaven fled away; and there was found no place for them.*
>
> Revelation 20:11

Williams' translation of this verse says, "Then I saw a white throne and Him who was seated on it from whose presence earth and sky fled away." This is most likely when the earth is burned by fire to be remade:

> *And the elements shall melt with fervent heat, the earth also and the works that are therein shall be burned up.*
>
> 2 Peter 3:10b

We now find the new earth and the new heaven, or atmosphere, of which we previously learned.

Inhabitants of the New Earth

On this remade earth, the New Jerusalem will descend to fit its spot on this planet forever. Since all those who refuse God are cast into the lake of fire, only two types of people remain with God in Heaven who will all descend together to inhabit the new earth.

The first are the glorified saints, who were part of the first resurrection. The second are the "natural" men and women who are still alive. After all, they lived through the millennium and sided with Jesus.

The glorified saints live in the New Jerusalem, while the natural people would populate the rest of the earth.

Natural Man's Purpose Restored

In the renewed earth, God restores with final authority the purpose and life of natural man and woman that He intended since the beginning of time.

No longer will demons hinder, or the devil deceive. So natural man will be able to know the joys of life on earth without satanic pressures or temptation.

If you can imagine how life would have been for Adam and Eve without sin or lucifer, then you can imagine the wonders of natural life on remade earth:

> *And I saw a new heaven and a new earth: for the first heaven and the first earth were passed away; and there was no more sea.*
>
> *And I John saw the holy city, new Jerusalem, coming down from God out of heaven, prepared as a bride adorned for her husband.*

And I heard a great voice out of heaven saying, Behold, the tabernacle of God is with men, and He will dwell with them, and they shall be His people, and God Himself shall be with them, and be their God.

And God shall wipe away all tears from their eyes; and there shall be no more death, neither sorrow, nor crying, neither shall there be any more pain: for the former things are passed away.

And He that sat upon the throne said, Behold, I make all things new. And He said unto me, Write: for these words are true and faithful.

Revelation 21:1-5

Eternal Life for Natural Man

Now that we better understand the sequence of final events, we can more readily see other truths from verses in chapter 21:

And the city had no need of the sun, neither of the moon, to shine in it: for the glory of God did lighten it, and the Lamb is the light thereof.

And the nations of them which are saved shall walk in the light of it: and the kings of the earth do bring their glory and honour into it.

And the gates of it shall not be shut at all by day: for there shall be no night there.

Revelation 21:23-25

Quite simply, the sun will remain for our natural man, but it is not needed in New Jerusalem. God's glory is brighter. However, God allows the privilege of walking in His light to the peoples of these saved nations as well as His glorified saints.

These people would also be free to come and walk the streets of the City of God. They may come and go as they wish. The gates are never closed. Their kings likewise bring the glory and honor of the nations into her borders forever.

We also gain new insight into these verses:

> *And he shewed me a pure river of water of life, clear as crystal, proceeding out of the throne of God and of the Lamb.*
>
> *In the midst of the street of it, and on either side of the river, was there the tree of life, which bare twelve manner of fruits, and yielded her fruit every month: and the leaves of the tree were for the healing of the nations.*
>
> Revelation 22:1-2

The leaves for the healing of the nations also would be for the natural saints upon the renewed earth. The glorified saints in the New Jerusalem certainly won't need healing!

That means the leaves on the trees in New Jerusalem will have a similar purpose as did the tree of life for Adam and Eve in the beginning. The leaves would preserve natural man's life forever.

Also, the word for "healing" mentioned in reference to these leaves is not the same word in Isaiah 53:5, "with His stripes we are healed." Rather, the word here means "preservation." Natural man's life would be preserved forever!

We know that if Adam had not sinned, God had physically created him to live forever. Even today we know that our physical bodies are capable of infinite life if not bound by pollution, the ravages of man's sin, and the penalty of death. Biologists know that about every seven years, our physical bodies completely renew themselves.

If natural man's full purpose is restored as we've discussed, then he would also plant crops, gather harvests, and build new houses and cities. He would multiply and replenish the earth just as Adam and his seed would have done if not for sin. They would marry and have children and repopulate the planet.

(In the next chapter we'll see more of how the Word of God says these things shall come to be.)

Life for Glorified Man

The Church, made up of the glorified saints, is to rule and reign with Christ as kings and priests forever (see Rev. 5:10). So it only makes sense that we would rule and reign with our King over the natural races of people in the new earth.

It wouldn't make much sense that we would rule over ourselves. It makes more sense to have "subjects" and "worshipers" if we are kings and priests. These would be natural man, over whom we administer the Kingdom of God on this new earth. We will represent our great God from His seat of power, the New Jerusalem, where we will live.

God tells us that our assignments will be rewards for the obedience and service we give now. It will take millions to fill every position in God's Kingdom—and we're that people. Man or woman, He created us to rule with authority in Him. The places to which He assigns us will fulfill a deep longing in each of us—a longing uniquely designed to enable us to become the ultimate person and likeness of whom He created us to be.

Moreover, we will have the honor to eternally worship Him. We will behold Him. We will praise and magnify Him. We will grow in the knowledge and the fullness of Him as we forever learn His ways. We will delight in all the good works He has prepared beforehand for us to do (see Eph. 2:10).

Be certain that anything we do for God and with God in Heaven will be more fulfilling than any position we ever held for a man. Our lives and purpose in Heaven will be more satisfying than any endeavor to which we have ever assigned ourselves. All we do will be in, through, and by the glorious, unhindered power of God Himself!

As Finis Dake best states in his work, *God's Plan for Man*:

> "One thing is sure. Whatever we do will be fulfilling and rewarding every single day. The fall of man did not cause God to change his original and eternal plan for man on earth. God cannot in the end suffer a defeat, so He turned man's fall into a blessing by His plan to gather out of the race during the period of the fall an heavenly people to reign over the natural people who will be redeemed from the fall, and all it effects, after the Millennium.
>
> "The Fall of man simply *delayed* the original purpose of God, but because of the delay God gained more than He would have gained otherwise."[1]

In other words, God was able to gain from it a "*heavenly resurrected and glorified people* who will reign over the coming generations of natural people." Without the fall of man, there would have been no people as the "Church" as we know it who will reign with Him forever.

What a privilege is extended to us. We are God's special people, a chosen people, a holy nation. By our allegiance to Christ now, we are called to be a ruling class with Christ's authority, chosen to administrate the Kingdom of God in eternity.

In His mercy and through the priceless gift of His Son, God has so fully redeemed us through salvation that we shall be ultimately untouched and unscathed by man's fall. We will be transformed so totally as His glorified saints that we will stand in oneness with Him. We will live with Him forever, clean and pure. In fact, we are so beautiful to Him that He has chosen us as His Bride...a joy that will abide through all ages!

So as we consider all the wondrous calling and hope that our God has set before us at the end of an age...how could we do anything other than worship and serve Him now!

Endnote

1. Finis Jennings Dake, *God's Plan for Man* (Lawrenceville, GA: Dake Bible Sales, Inc., 1949, 1977), 992-993.

Chapter 13

Life on the New Earth

Imagine the beauty of the remade Earth, free from the torment and ravage of sin. Imagine the home of the New Jerusalem, and of restored natural man.

Once again, the Word of God tells us much about this renewed planet and what her residents will be doing. A covenant God doesn't do things one way for one era, and then another for another time. His constants will again be found in how life will be.

As we mentioned in the previous chapter, outside of New Jerusalem, natural man would begin to replenish the earth. He would live a normal life as natural man by growing crops and harvesting them, building homes and cities to live in, and working in whatever industries are necessary to life.

Even though natural man labors and provides for his family, he would be marvelously free of the constraints (caused by sin) under which his predecessors strived. No longer would he work by the "sweat of his brow." His labor shall not be in worry or strain!

It would be just as it would have been for Adam had he never sinned. A great part of man's delight and worth comes from pursuing his life purpose or work. God designed us this way. From the very beginning, Adam had been placed in the garden to dress and keep it, and to name the animals (see Gen. 2:15,19).

These endeavors were to be a joy and a fulfillment. The Hebrew for "dress" is *abad*, meaning "to work or labor." To "keep" is *shamar*, meaning to "tend over it"; to "hedge around it."

Thus, Adam was to work the garden and tend to its care. Originally he did so without anxiety or pressure. He was intended to be a provider, yet that provision was to yield joys and rewards along with productivity.

After Adam fell into sin, thorns and thistles sprang up, and the earth no longer produced its potential. Man then made his living by the "sweat of his brow" (see Gen. 3:19).

In the new earth, we've suggested that natural man will be as Adam was before his fall. There'll be no thorns, thistles, or weeds: no sweat! Both man and the earth he tends will no longer suffer or miss their full potential. Work will be fulfilling, not tormenting.

Likewise, the glorified saints will be satisfied and blessed in their chosen callings as they administrate the government of the Kingdom of God. We will be consummately occupied as we rule and reign with Christ over natural man, the earth, the universe, and the angels (see 1 Cor. 6:3).

Populating the Earth

The fascinating close to the Book of Revelation poses some interesting possibilities and questions. Of course, we will know more after one hour in Heaven than we could possibly speculate at this time. Yet there are some answers we can theorize now.

The question arises about marriage and populating the earth. Will there be children in the new earth? If so, doesn't the Bible say that there is no marriage in Heaven?

Just as before, we must consider the biblical context. The verses on marriage that Jesus spoke in Mark's Gospel would not apply to natural people in Heaven, but to glorified saints:

> *Then come unto Him the Sadducees, which say there is no resurrection; and they asked Him, saying,*
>
> *Master, Moses wrote unto us, If a man's brother die, and leave his wife behind him, and leave no children, that his brother should take his wife, and raise up seed unto his brother.*
>
> *Now there were seven brethren: and the first took a wife, and dying left no seed.*
>
> *And the second took her, and died, neither left he any seed: and the third likewise.*
>
> *And the seven had her, and left no seed: last of all the woman died also.*
>
> *In the resurrection therefore, when they shall rise, whose wife shall she be of them? for the seven had her to wife.*
>
> *And Jesus answering said unto them, Do ye not therefore err, because ye know not the scriptures, neither the power of God?*

For when they shall rise from the dead, they neither marry, nor are given in marriage; but are as the angels which are in heaven.

Mark 12:18-25

Jesus is clearly speaking about those who rise from the dead in the first resurrection, or the rapture. These people will not marry or give in marriage. Yet it only makes sense that natural man who lived through the millennium will repopulate the renewed earth.

If that is true, then there would be sexual relationships in the new heaven and the new earth. As to whether glorified saints will participate in such relationships with their spouses, we simply do not know.

We do know that our relationships with our husbands and wives will be more fulfilling and complete than they are now. What that entails is not entirely clear. There is a mystery about it that God has not yet revealed.

It does seem clear that we will know our spouses in Heaven if they are born again. The Scriptures tell of great times of reunion and fellowship that are restored to families. It only makes sense that a covenant God would not allow such a vital covenant relationship to be dissolved in Heaven.

Most likely, we will find that a family covenant bond will exist and even be enhanced. Since we don't know all the details, we will just have to trust God for what is to come, knowing it will be excellent and satisfying. With what we've seen of God's promises already, is that so hard to do?

It has probably not even entered our minds how great and fulfilling all aspects of eternal relationships will be. Although it is beyond our understanding to know it now, every physical, mental, emotional, and spiritual element of relationships will be far superior in our glorified eternal lives.

To some degree, we can also understand what life would be like for the natural man from the saved nations since we have been natural men. Yet what God has in store for the Church must be so far beyond it, He doesn't even try to explain it now!

God has kept for later the full disclosure of the wonders and delights that await us for eternity!

Eternal Wonders

Many of us have suffered loss or pain in relationships here, and may have a hard time even envisioning the joy of restoration in Heaven.

Yet to think that God cannot do something far more wonderful within families or the husband-wife relationship than the best of what we've known here is contrary to His nature!

Our majestic, awesome, creative God has so much more in mind.

If He can boggle our minds with the walls and gates of New Jerusalem, imagine what He can do with our relationships. If the streets and fruits of Heaven are beyond comprehension, imagine our communion with our family and loved ones who have called upon His name. The premise of His whole creation is relationship!

Take hope in the healing and restoration. Imagine the amplified love and care within families. It would have to be incredibly brilliant—and be forever new. We would live in His own *agape* love, which never ends, becomes obsolete or old, or fades. This love is the very essence of God Himself, and would follow us throughout time.

That means our relationships would daily grow toward their true purpose and fulfillment. They would be eternal gain to us. All that we could not do or be in our finite state He would weave within us as He brings us to completion.

To think that Heaven will not excite or fulfill us is to negate the skill of our God to satisfy and make complete. Based on who He is and what He has promised, no doubt we will be continually amazed and astonished at the unfathomable riches of our God.

Eternity itself will not be enough time to discover it all!

A Few Practicals

Even the most inspired aspirant to Heaven may still be thinking about how the "practicals" will be resolved in the new earth and New Jerusalem.

Wouldn't it be awesome for God's original plan to be carried out, with the natural man marrying, producing children, and replenishing the earth?

Yet if our natural man does multiply on the earth, will we eventually run out of room in a few million years?

Habitable Space

As we discussed briefly in Chapter 10, there will be no more seas in the new earth (see Rev. 21:1).

Consider this in more detail. In the new earth, the oceans will be done away with, opening a vast expanse of land that would become habitable. We are told the earth is approximately 196,950,000 square miles. Granting that there will be no more oceans, only rivers, streams, and lakes, that means most of that total acreage would be available.

Finis J. Dake, in his work, *God's Plan for Man*, foresees no population dilemma based on his calculations, which are as follows: Allow 4,650,000 square miles for rivers, streams, and lakes. (This is no doubt a high guess.) Then allow 2,250,000 square miles for New Jerusalem itself because it is 1500 miles square. If you deduct all that from 196,650,000, you have 190,000,000 square miles for man to live outside of New Jerusalem.

If you gave one acre to every person, you would have room for 121,600,000,000 people. Of course, right now there are approximately five billion people on earth, which means that on the new earth there is room for 116,600,000,000 more people than we have now.[1]

Childbirth

Of course, with that kind of room available for that many more people, the question of habitable space probably won't arise anytime soon.

However, central to this idea is scriptural evidence that suggests population growth itself will be slowed. According to Genesis, multiple pregnancies and the accompanying distress were a result of man's fall:

> *...I will greatly multiply thy sorrow and thy conception; in sorrow thou shalt bring forth children....*
>
> Genesis 3:16

The sorrow of childbirth refers to the pain and labor a woman experiences when giving birth. Yet God says He will multiply also "thy conception." The Hebrew word for "conception" is *herown*, meaning "pregnancy." Therefore, God is saying pregnancies will now be multiplied.

In the new earth, the fall has been dealt with and God's original purposes are restored. It seems it was originally God's plan for man to only duplicate himself. Thus, each couple would have only one or two children, thereby reproducing only their own images. We can't know this for sure, but it has great merit.

If this is so, then in the new earth, when the penalties of pain and multiple pregnancies are removed, natural man would most likely multiply at a slower pace. There will be room for billions of people.

Of course, should the size of the earth limit God's plans for expansion, He could easily open up the universe. Other planets could be remade as easily as the planet Earth. We'll simply have to wait and see if what we suppose about natural man comes to pass!

Time

If natural man will live forever upon remade Earth, will there be time as we know it? If natural man lives among us, there would have to be. Consider the evidence.

God has made time to march on throughout eternity. The Greek word for "eternal" is *aionios*, meaning "perpetual time." Perpetual time includes forever past and forever future time, as well as time never ending.

It is important to understand that eternity does not begin when you get to Heaven. It actually begins for you when you are conceived. That means that you are already living in eternity! Eternity has more to do with time than it does with place, a concept confusing to some.

The fact is that you will live forever somewhere—either in Heaven or hell. Time will continue. There will be 24 hours in a day, 60 minutes in an hour, 60 seconds in a minute. There will be seasons regulated by the sun, moon, and stars.

Again, our covenant God has made certain "absolutes" to remain. Your "change of place" to be an inhabitant of the New Jerusalem will not change those absolutes—which include time.

The Scriptures enforce this truth:

> *While the earth remaineth, seedtime and harvest, and cold and heat, and summer and winter, and day and night shall not cease.*
>
> Genesis 8:22

There will still be seasons and time on the new earth.

Likewise, Psalm 89 shares one of God's eternal promises to David:

> *His seed also will I make to endure for ever.*
>
> Psalm 89:29a

"Forever" in this context is the word *ad* in the Hebrew. *Ad* means forever time, the duration of forever time, or eternity. In effect, this verse says that God will make David's descendents to endure forever throughout all eternity, and His covenant will stand fast with them.

A few verses further in the same Psalm, the Lord says:

My covenant will I not break, nor alter the thing that is gone out of my lips.

Once have I sworn by My holiness that I will not lie unto David.

His seed shall endure for ever, and his throne as the sun before Me.

It shall be established for ever as the moon, and as a faithful witness in heaven. Selah.

Psalm 89:34-37

Each "forever" in these verses is likewise *ad*, meaning throughout eternity. God promises that David's descendents will never cease to be in existence on the earth. They will live in "forever" time. Therefore, we believe that David's own descendents will comprise a portion of the natural men and women who are to replenish the new earth, thus fulfilling God's everlasting covenant to him.

Another question that may arise stems from Revelation, wherein a promise is made that there will be "no more time":

And sware by Him that liveth for ever and ever, who created heaven, and the things that therein are, and the earth, and the things that therein are, and the sea, and the things which are therein, that there should be time no longer.

Revelation 10:6

Again, the important issue is context. "Time" in this verse is the Greek *chronos*, meaning a "space of time," a "measurement of time," or a "length of time."

This verse is simply saying that the length of time allowed at this point is finished or complete. This reference speaks of a dispensation of allotted time. An example would be taking an exam. If you have only one hour to complete the test, at the end of that hour, you would have run out of "time." That is *chronos* time, or one allotment. It does not mean that all time as we know it stops.

Other translations of this same verse support the *chronos* context. The Amplified Bible states, "that no more time should intervene and there should be no more waiting or delay." The Revised Standard Version says, "that there should be no more delay."

In other words, time is up for this purpose of God to happen, and there will be no more time given to delay God's purpose.

Dr. Hilton Sutton, in his Revelation Seminar (page 29 of the notebook) explains that this verse is set in the midst of the tribulation period, which is seven years long. The messenger angel is simply saying, "Don't delay any longer. Let's get with it and speed up what is left to come."

We know that time itself does not stop here because the very next verse in Revelation talks about the "days ahead." Days are time! We also know that the rest of the tribulation must come to pass, as well as the 1,000-year millennial reign. "Years" again refer to time!

Thus, there are spaces of time (chronos) that will end, but not time itself. The space of time for man in this dimension—before the last judgment—is coming to an end. This end will not be prolonged or delayed. We shall then enter "forever" time.

Learning

Understanding the concept of eternal time helps us answer another important question about learning. Many people feel that we will "instantly know everything" as soon as we get to Heaven.

Some base their case on a popular verse of First Corinthians: "Now I know in part; but then shall I know [fully] even as also I am known" (1 Cor. 13:12b).

This, however, does not follow with what other things God says await us in New Jerusalem. The fact that the fruit trees of Heaven bear fruit every month means there still remains a passage of time required for productivity. Although the process is greatly accelerated (fruit is borne in about a fourth of the time required now), time is still necessary.

Likewise, God has created a desire to learn. This desire is one of the most satisfying of all drives. There is great fulfillment in the learning process—and a process, by definition, requires time. It makes more sense that we will be forever learning, even if the time and the effort required are less than we know now.

Waiting

The whole concept of waiting will be changed in Heaven. Yes, we will have to wait on certain things to come to pass. Yet it will not be the impatient waiting we experience now. It will be an excited period of expectation for what the passage of time continues to bring our way.

The Lord's nature is that of continual productivity, expectation, and satisfaction; so too shall be the waiting. There will still be seconds and minutes and days and years as time marches on forever. But we will experience time and waiting without the tedium of the aging process and the feeling that life is passing us by.

Every second will be filled with meaning—and life more abundant and new with our God. We'll forever increase in His joy and knowledge as time goes forth!

Gain

For to me to live is Christ, and to die is gain.

But if I live in the flesh, this is the fruit of my labour: yet what I shall choose I wot not.

For I am in a strait betwixt two, having a desire to depart, and to be with Christ; which is far better.

Philippians 1:21-23

Even though God has made marvels for us to enjoy now in this earth, Heaven will be far superior. There will be no comparison. To live without the constraints of sin and in His eternal presence will be a privilege and a joy man has never known before. Yet it seems as though few people actually believe this!

Too many are bent on feverish labors here, believing that nothing more will follow. Do you live as though you will see the reality of Heaven?

In his work, *Probing Heaven*, John Gilmore says many Christians act "like functional atheists."[2] In other words, their life and their mental attitudes do not reflect so great a promise of Heaven.

John Rice, in *Bible Facts About Heaven*, sees it this way: "We feel that Heaven is bearable, all right, when one has sucked dry all the pleasures of earth. We feel that, only after old age has come upon us, when life is a burden, when health has failed, when we are in the way and our children don't want us, then perhaps we should be resigned to go to Heaven...."[3]

He urges us to more readily consider that "death is not a tragedy, but a glorious promotion. Not a sad end, but the glorious beginning."[4]

The truth is that to die is gain for the Christian. This does not mean we are to seek death as quickly as possible. The apostle Paul was not thinking that when he said dying was gain. He knew that he should stay and continue his work for God, but there was no question in his mind about which option was more desirable.

Paul knew that Heaven was far better than anything this earth could offer. He desired Heaven deep in his heart. He longed to be with Christ far more than he wanted to stay. That is the perspective God intends for each of us! This earth is not our home!

It is not that we become so "heavenly minded" that we are no earthly good. It is the exact opposite. It is that we become eternally effective, knowing with all confidence that we have a better place to go to than this old world.

Then, with our hearts and minds set like flint toward the beautiful City of God, the New Jerusalem, we continue to minister the gospel of our King in this life. We continue our labor of love and service toward unregenerate man and one another.

Rather than our occupations, our positions, our possessions, our money, our houses and lands, or our earthly lives becoming our number one goal, they become secondary goals for those who truly understand and believe God's Word.

They become secondary to our firm hope of one day marching through the gates of pearl and walking down golden broadways to Mount Zion, where we shall behold our God face to face. They become secondary to meeting Jesus Christ, our beloved Lord and Master. They pale in comparison to receiving the directions to our new residence in that city of gold, and the eternal fulfillment and joys that will be ours forever.

Living Now

It is time we showed the world that we really believe the Bible. It's time we show them we believe that Heaven is real—and that we have something worth living for, worth working for, and worth dying for.

This world is not our final home; we are just passing through here. Heaven is indeed a far better place than the world could ever offer. It is time we live like we understand that Heaven is gain to the Christian.

In Heaven we shall gain access to all that God is, to the entire universe, to perfect health, to uninterrupted peace, to wealth beyond imagination, to incorruptible treasures, to unspoiled beauty. We gain access to God Himself forever!

Living in this confident expectation would allow a victorious Church to demonstrate reality to the world in her final days upon this earth.

Living in this confident expectation would change the way you live for Christ every day of your life!

We would give our "all" for Him—knowing there is great reward! We would spend our last ounce of energy and enthusiasm serving Him and sharing the truth with others.

There is coming a day when those who have labored so diligently on this earth will receive that glorious promise of eternal rest and of the presence of God Himself. It will be a day when all labor will be rewarded, and that one day will be worth it all. It will be a day like no other—a day of endless gain!

Endnotes

1. Finis Jennings Dake, *God's Plan for Man* (Lawrenceville, GA: Dake Bible Sales, Inc., 1949, 1977), 996-997.

2. John Gilmore, *Probing Heaven* (Grand Rapids, MI: Baker Book House, 1989), 58.

3. John R. Rice, *Bible Facts About Heaven* (Murfreesboro, TN: Sword of the Lord Publishers, 1940), 38.

4. Rice, *Bible Facts*, 38.

Chapter 14

Rewards and Seeing Jesus as He Is

The Book of Revelation concludes with Christ stating three times, "I come quickly," and one stement, "The time is at hand."

> *And he said unto me, These sayings are faithful and true: and the Lord God of the holy prophets sent His angel to shew unto His servants the things which must shortly be done.*
>
> *Behold,* **I come quickly***: blessed is he that keepeth the sayings of the prophecy of this book.*
>
> *And I John saw these things, and heard them. And when I had heard and seen, I fell down to worship before the feet of the angel which shewed me these things.*
>
> *Then saith he unto me, See thou do it not: for I am thy fellowservant, and of thy brethren the prophets, and of them which keep the sayings of this book: worship God.*

And he saith unto me, Seal not the sayings of the prophecy of this book: ***for the time is at hand.***

He that is unjust, let him be unjust still: and he which is filthy, let him be filthy still: and he that is righteous, let him be righteous still: and he that is holy, let him be holy still.

And, behold, ***I come quickly****; and My reward is with Me, to give every man according as his work shall be.*

I am Alpha and Omega, the beginning and the end, the first and the last.

Blessed are they that do His commandments, that they may have right to the tree of life, and may enter in through the gates into the city.

For without are dogs, and sorcerers, and whore-mongers, and murderers, and idolaters, and whoso-ever loveth and maketh a lie.

I Jesus have sent Mine angel to testify unto you these things in the churches. I am the root and the offspring of David, and the bright and morning star.

And the Spirit and the bride say, Come. And let him that heareth say, Come. And let him that is athirst come. And whosoever will, let him take the water of life freely.

For I testify unto every man that heareth the words of the prophecy of this book, If any man shall add unto these things, God shall add unto him the plagues that are written in this book:

And if any man shall take away from the words of the book of this prophecy, God shall take away his part out of the book of life, and out of the holy city, and from the things which are written in this book.

He which testifieth these things saith, ***Surely I come quickly****. Amen. Even so, come, Lord Jesus.*

The grace of our Lord Jesus Christ be with you all. Amen.

Revelation 22:6-21

Although it may not seem all that quick to man, keep in mind that the One making this statement has and will live forever. Millions of years are nothing to our God. In fact, 2,000 years would elapse rather quickly for Him!

The *chronos* time or the space of time allotted to the duration of this planet is much closer to ending today than at any other time. This is truly the midnight hour for the earth!

The dawn of a new century may not hold any promise of another hundred years. When you consider history, more has happened in the last few years than the last hundred: the Berlin Wall, Russia, the United States of Europe, natural disasters and calamity, the evangelization of the planet, the state of man, etc.

Undeniably, Jesus is coming soon. He is telling the Church, His Bride, to get ready. We are to allow God to rid us of our spots and wrinkles that He might present to Himself a glorious Church. As Christ's coming is upon us, He has left us clear direction regarding the purpose of our efforts while we wait:

And, behold, I come quickly; and ***My reward is with Me, to give every man according as his work shall be.***

Revelation 22:12

God never intended that our wait be idle. Rather, the Word of God has always made it clear that our *reward* in Heaven will be based on what we accomplish in Him on this earth!

This does not mean our salvation is based upon works or that our entrance to Heaven is dependent upon them. Every Christian who acknowledges Jesus as Lord will not only receive salvation, but also entrance to Heaven.

This verse is simply saying that every person will be *rewarded* in Heaven based on services rendered here. The Greek word for "reward" is *misthos*, meaning "wages, pay for services, payments for deeds, or payment for work."

The Greek for "work" is *ergon*, meaning "performance" or "labor." *Ergon* is generally used to describe "acts that prove the genuine nature of our faith." That translates to acts of service that prove we believe God. It also means "how" someone acts.

Thus, even though our salvation is not based on performance, our rewards most definitely are! This certainly gives us more clarity for motive and service now rather than any justification for idle time.

Rewards

The Bible is filled with promptings for us to "be all we can be." God intends for us to make the most of the glorious talents and gifts He has invested in us. Not only does our fulfillment on earth depend greatly on the degree to which we are so occupied, but so does our eternal return as well.

Although you may not go to hell for hiding your talents, you will not be rewarded the same as if you had employed them. If you do not serve the Kingdom of God on earth in the measure with which the Holy Spirit prompts you, getting to Heaven is not the issue. Your reward in Heaven is!

It would not be fair for you to receive the same heavenly privileges that others have if you are not willing to obey God's prompting. For example, you cannot expect the same reward as those who selflessly teach, sing, or serve if God has asked that of you, yet you do not respond. Nor can you receive the same reward as those who give when you withhold.

It may appear that God does not notice such detail, but the records of Heaven are very specific—to the point that even giving a cup of water makes the grade:

> *And whosoever shall give to drink...a cup of cold water...verily I say unto you, he shall in no wise lose his reward.*
>
> Matthew 10:42

Likewise, Jesus said, "If you receive a prophet, you receive a prophet's reward" (see Mt. 10:41). To "receive" in this context means to "be hospitable."

That means if you show hospitality to a prophet, you will receive a prophet's payment for service rendered. Likewise, if you receive a righteous man, you will receive a righteous man's reward (see Mt. 10:41).

Our God will reward the most minute acts of kindness, down to a pat on the back! How much more will He reward faithful, obedient service for a lifetime!

Eternal Perspective

To better understand the reward God offers you for eternity, consider the following proposition: If you were offered a job today that would last five full minutes, but promised you eternal rewards for billions of years, would you work it gladly?

If effect, that is what God has asked of us in our limited time upon this earth. Compared to eternity's promises, our 50 or 60 years of potential service on this planet is, at best, only five minutes. Perhaps it is more like a millionth of a second!

Doubtless, no man on earth would spend that last five minutes in selfish endeavors or sitting idle. He would invest in his full five minutes for that eternal return.

However, many people do not invest their lives because they fail to believe that God "is a rewarder of them that diligently seek Him" (Heb. 11:6). They are "too busy" for the things of God. They completely forget what eternal time is going to add, and they only live for here and now. They miss the truth of Heaven's reward.

Many people are similarly deceived into thinking that Christianity is effortless and costs us nothing. Nowhere in the Scriptures can we find this as a description of the true faith.

The rewards of Heaven should sober one who is wise. We cannot mock God, live a selfish and lazy life, and still expect a reward. The truth is that God will not tolerate such foolishness!

> *And cast ye the unprofitable servant into outer darkness: there shall be weeping and gnashing of teeth.*
>
> Matthew 25:30

God must judge those who unwisely spend their lives and talents, for He is a fair and just God. Willing service in God's Kingdom is therefore not only rewarded; it is expected.

Don't make the mistake of some who think they'll settle for the least "cabin" in Heaven because it would be better than anything in hell. You might not get the opportunity!

God expects the Bride to show her love for the Bridegroom, Jesus. That means giving outward, selfless service to the Kingdom of God, His heart's desire.

Many today mistakenly call service to themselves or to their own families the work of God. It is true that God asks this attention of us, but it can be merely serving ourselves. God has asked us to serve the Church, to do His work upon the whole earth. It is naive or self-absorbed of us to do otherwise. The measure of our reward is clear.

The 20th Century New Testament says, "Christ will come and give to every man what his actions deserve" (Rev. 22:12). The Revised Standard Version states, "to repay every one for what he has done." Knox's translation reads, "repaying each man according to the life he has lived."

We must take an inward look and consider how we spend our lives and to what we give ourselves. The Gospel of Matthew exhorts:

> *Lay not up for yourselves treasures upon earth, where moth and rust doth corrupt, and where thieves break through and steal:*
>
> *But lay up for yourselves treasures in heaven, where neither moth nor rust doth corrupt, and where thieves do not break through nor steal:*

For where your treasure is, there will your heart be also.

Matthew 6:19-21

Treasure Ahead

All of us have heard it said before that no matter what we accumulate now, we "can't take it with us." That means the millionaire will not pack his money in the casket when he departs. His money will serve him no purpose in Heaven. However, that same man could have laid up true treasures.

God has purposed that each of us have the opportunity to lay up lasting treasures for that day when we arrive in Heaven.

That means we need to exercise wise stewardship of the life He has given us, diligent service, and obedience to God's Word. Why invest our lives in things that moths and rust will eventually take in this life, when we can invest in rewards that will forever yield a return?

The Greek word for "lay up" literally means to "amass, to store up." Jesus made it clear that we should "amass our treasure in Heaven."

Consider it this way: Let's say you know that in two years you will be moving overseas for a job change, and that you can't take anything with you. However, you are permitted to send anything you like ahead of your departure.

Certainly you would do this! You would spend your time now planning what you wanted and sending it ahead. Yet again, many people do not believe they truly can lay up treasure in Heaven, so they send nothing.

Storing up your heavenly reward does not have to mean living the life of an ascetic here and giving away all you own. God has a purpose for prosperity in this life too. It simply means you are to focus on the treasure you can gain for Heaven that will never spoil or disappoint.

Even the poorest person on this earth can have the promise of the richest future as he gains the treasures that will never fade.

The Bible gives us a number of examples of treasures we can store:

Sharing the joy of salvation (Dan. 12:3). The greatest reward will be those you bring with you to Heaven. Sharing the good news of the gospel is our number one purpose on the earth, and indeed, those who "turn many to righteousness" will shine "as the stars for ever and ever."

Prayer (Mt. 6:6). A prayer offered in secret will be rewarded openly. The prayer for a child, a neighbor, the Church, or the world adds to your storehouse of blessings in Heaven.

Faithfulness (Mt. 25:23). Faith without works is dead! (See James 2:17, 26.) Show yourself faithful to do the things of God and you too will hear Him say, "Well done, good and faithful servant; thou hast been faithful over a few things, I will make thee ruler over many things: enter thou into the joy of thy lord." That is quite a reward!

Giving to the poor (Mt. 6:4). As you supply food, goods, and funds to the poor, God Himself will reward you. Whether you support your local food bank, church outreach, homeless shelter, clothing drive, or international mission, God takes account.

Loving your enemies (Lk. 6:35). Responding like Christ to those who hate you carries not just a good reward, but a *great* reward. Show His nature to all and you will be blessed forever.

Fasting (Mt. 6:18). As you deny yourself on behalf of God and His Church to be about His business, it is multiplied to your treasures.

Suffering persecution for the gospel (Mt. 5:11-12). Standing true to God's Word in the midst of being reviled and others speaking evil of you is special to God's heart. It will also be rewarded greatly. Suffer reproach gladly, for it is surely added to your chest of treasures!

Again, salvation is not determined by our works, but our rewards are. Our status in New Jerusalem will be based on what is written to our account. Even the least among us can do something. With God, faithfulness in the smallest things adds up to greatness. Whatever it is, whatever He is asking of you, put your hand to do it mightily (see Eccles. 9:10). Do not faint or grow weary, but give your life to sending your treasures on ahead!

Rank

Though some may find it offensive to think of "rank" in Heaven, all throughout the Word of God we find differing levels of accomplishment and reward.

God talks about those people whose lives yield a 30, 60, or 100-fold return on the Word of God (see Mt. 13:23);

likewise, it speaks of those who are "greatest" and "least" in the Kingdom (Mt. 5:19).

There will also be the same delineation in Heaven. Of course, there will be no "second class citizens." But in terms of greatness, there will be different measures. Your position and rank will forever be determined by the brief years of service you have now. It is in your hands, through the power of God, to determine your due.

The status of servants who work hard now will be far greater than those who do nothing. More will be given to the workers. To all who have ever wondered, "I do all I can. I give and I serve. It seems so few others help, and when will there be a reward?" God is saying there is coming a day when the scales will be tipped, and you will receive your due. Be patient and rejoice, for your reward is sure!

Greater authority and rule is a major part of that greater reward for those who serve now. The apostle Paul made this clear when he wrote to Timothy shortly before being beheaded in Rome:

> *For I am now ready to be offered, and the time of my departure is at hand.*
>
> *I have fought a good fight, I have finished my course, I have kept the faith:*
>
> *Henceforth there is laid up for me a crown of righteousness, which the Lord, the righteous judge, shall give me at that day: and not to me only, but unto all them also that love His appearing.*
>
> 2 Timothy 4:6-8

Every one of us has the same privilege of participating in God's reward system. Choosing to do so is up to us. Wisdom and the shortness of time say to get involved now with the Bride. Serve the Church of Jesus Christ today and share His love and truth with all the world!

His Promise

Jesus Himself has already prayed for your success on earth in being about His Father's business. He has further asked that, as your reward, you be with Him in Heaven and behold His glory (see Jn. 17:9-26).

From what we have learned of Heaven, that is some promise. There are notable absences in the New Jerusalem and the new earth. There are no funeral homes, no cemeteries, no doctors' offices, no fire or police departments, no hospitals or psychiatric facilities. Nor are there insurance agencies, attorneys' offices, or income tax facilities. Instead there is a place of indescribable beauty and fulfillment.

Moreover, we shall be with Him. We shall behold Him in His glory! Not a frail king, weakened by the cross. Not a man beset by nails and thorns and scorn. But a risen Savior, in all His power and majesty, just as when He spoke the world into being.

John gives us a glimpse of that day, notwithstanding his own confinement to prison, as he wrote:

> *I John, who also am your brother, and companion in tribulation, and in the kingdom and patience of Jesus Christ, was in the isle that is called Patmos, for the word of God, and for the testimony of Jesus Christ.*

I was in the Spirit on the Lord's day, and heard behind me a great voice, as of a trumpet,

Saying, I am Alpha and Omega, the first and the last: and, What thou seest, write in a book, and send it unto the seven churches which are in Asia; unto Ephesus, and unto Smyrna, and unto Pergamos, and unto Thyatira, and unto Sardis, and unto Philadelphia, and unto Laodicea.

And I turned to see the voice that spake with me. And being turned, I saw seven golden candlesticks;

And in the midst of the seven candlesticks one like unto the Son of man, clothed with a garment down to the foot, and girt about the paps with a golden girdle.

His head and His hairs were white like wool, as white as snow; and His eyes were as a flame of fire;

And His feet like unto fine brass, as if they burned in a furnace; and His voice as the sound of many waters.

And He had in His right hand seven stars: and out of His mouth went a sharp twoedged sword: and His countenance was as the sun shineth in His strength. [The Amplified Bible says, "His face was like the sun shining in full power at midday"!]

And when I saw Him, I fell at His feet as dead. And He laid His right hand upon me, saying unto me, Fear not; I am the first and the last:

I am He that liveth, and was dead; and, behold, I am alive for evermore, Amen; and have the keys of hell and of death.

Revelation 1:9-18

That is the Jesus we are going to see in Heaven. That is the King of the universe we shall forever behold! He is a matchless, majestic God in His glorious surroundings with all the angels and the full host of Heaven!

> *Now over the heads of the living beings there was something like an expanse. There was a firmament over them like the awesome gleam of transparent crystal. It extended over their heads. And under the expanse I heard the sound of their wings, like the sound of roaring rushing waters, like the sound of an excited army camp.*
>
> *And over the expanse, I heard a voice speaking. And looking over the living beings, and out over the shimmering seas of transparent, crystal-clear gold, I saw something resembling a throne. It was a throne made of clear blue sapphires. And upon the throne, high and lifted up, was the Son of God.*
>
> *His appearance was amber-colored, and His loins and upwards glowed like metal in a fire. His loins downward glowed like flames of fire. There was brilliant radiance exuding off of Him. The radiance appeared in the form of a rainbow after the rain, so that all around Him and His throne, His glory appeared in the form of rainbow colors.*
>
> Ezekial 1:22-28 (my paraphrase)

Oh, what a day that will be! Ezekial saw the Lord on a beautiful sapphire throne. The rainbow colors shimmered and danced off the expansive gold floors of God's throne room. John also saw the same God of glory, whose appearing was just like a jasper stone with an emerald rainbow around the throne (see Rev. 4:2-3).

Yes, it is coming and will not delay. Now we see through a glass darkly, and our relationship and revelation of our infinite Savior is limited by our finite minds.

Soon we shall behold Him face to face and see His splendor. Our vile bodies will be fashioned like unto His glorious body; we shall be caught up in the air. Our fellowship with Him shall never again know limitations. We shall embrace the King of kings and Lord of lords in unbroken, unhindered, unstoppable, unobstructed, unimpeded communion forever!

Set your sight on that day. Live your life for that eternity. Remember, the earth is not your home. It is Heaven that is real!

Come Quickly

Consider as a final note this account of an important moment in the life of missionary H.C. Morrison. Returning from a grueling missionary journey, he traveled on the same ship as President Teddy Roosevelt, who had been on an African safari.

As the ship pulled into port, thousands of enthusiastic, screaming supporters with huge banners welcomed the President home from his time of personal recreation.

A dejected H.C. Morrison noticed that not one person was on the dock to meet him. Exhausted and lonely, Morrison stood silently by. He said to the Lord, "God, I have been out serving You and telling all that I could about Jesus. I have been in hot, sweaty deserts and suffered many hardships. I have gone without sleep and without food, and I am worn out. And yet not one person has come to greet me. Not one person has come to welcome me home."

At that point, he recounts that he heard the voice of the Lord ever so clearly say, "But son, you're not home yet."

Remember, the best is yet to come. You too are not home yet. The rewards and the promise of Heaven are sure. Even so, come quickly, Lord Jesus!

Appendix

People's Experiences of Heaven

About Our Appearance in Heaven

Yvonne:

My baby brother died at 11 hours old when I was only three. Because I was so young and had never met him or seen him, I never really thought much about what he would look like over the years since then.

When my father died at a relatively young 67, the strangest thing happened. I remember leaving the hospital and heading down the road in the car. I was crying out to God for comfort, and I had the most amazing vision.

I saw my father just arriving in Heaven and walking toward a whole group of people that he seemed to know. I believe they were his parents, grandparents, and family that had gone on before him. Suddenly, one young man stepped forth and took my daddy's hand. He asked Daddy if he knew who he was, and my daddy said no. The young man introduced himself as his son—and they warmly embraced each other.

In my vision my baby brother had grown up in Heaven. Even though it had been 40 years since his death, he seemed to be around 30 or so years of age in my vision.

The last thing I was thinking about at the time of my daddy's death was the brother I had never met—but God in His kindness let me share that moment as it seemed to happen for my daddy! When a friend shared with me the idea that people in Heaven will most likely appear "thirty something," I had to agree because this is just how my brother appeared in that vision.

Jeanie:

I was thanking God that He took my father by a very peaceful death at the age of 92. Two weeks after he died, I was praying and wondering if my dad, a very private man, was in Heaven. As I was caught up in the spirit, I saw my dad. He was a young man with dark black hair. He was in Heaven, and was in his 30's. He had white hair when he died. Now he appeared so different. I knew this meant he was with the Lord.

Vickie Lynn:

During a sermon on Heaven, the Lord allowed me to see a vision of my baby girl, whom I had miscarried four years earlier, as she was in Heaven. She had shoulder-length brown hair and green eyes. She was running with the other children in a golden field of what looked like wheat—laughing and playing. She looked just like her sister Lindsey, who has just turned five. Yet at the time of the vision, Lindsey hadn't been born yet!

Claire:

During the time I was attending a post-abortion Bible study, we were encouraged to ask God for a vision of our children who had been aborted and to name them to help in our own healing and release. I had always felt in my heart that my baby I had aborted 18 years before had been a boy, and I named him "Brian."

That evening, while I was seeking God, the Holy Spirit reminded me of Isaiah 54:13. The version of the Bible that I opened and read said, "And all thy sons shall be taught of the Lord; and great shall be the peace of thy sons." As I was weeping thankful tears for the confirmation, I actually caught a glimpse in my spirit of a tall young man with dark hair being taught by Jesus Himself. My remorse has now been exchanged for joy, knowing what God has done.

Ruby:

I was at a Bible study when we received a call that our good friend had died. All the ladies started crying except me! I couldn't cry because I saw her running up a beautiful green hill. She looked as if she was 20 years old with a perfect complexion. All the hair she had lost during cancer treatments was replaced with long, flowing, shiny black hair. She was so vibrant and smiling. I could hear her saying, "I'm free, I'm free!" as she ran and ran. She was running to meet the Master!

Charles:

My father died of cancer in 1991. He was totally gray-headed, had very poor vision from diabetes, and was bloated from chemotherapy. He gave his heart to Jesus just three hours before he passed away. He said he was at peace.

About a week later, I had two dreams on two consecutive nights. In these dreams, my father looked to be about 40 and in perfect health. His hair was brown as it had been before, he was slim and trim, and did not wear or need glasses…

…In the second dream, Dad was casually walking down a path through a lush valley in a forest. He was the picture of health. He was walking to meet a host of people waiting to receive him. Some I did not recognize, but others were clearly family members who had passed away earlier….

Maxine:

When my uncle died, I was unable to attend his funeral, and I felt very bad about that. The evening of his funeral, I was at a praise and worship service. As I was worshiping in the Spirit, God showed me Uncle Curt running and jumping in Heaven. He looked so happy, and younger. That was far better than seeing him in a casket. I thank God for that vision….

Jeanne:

My father lived and enjoyed most of his 93 years. He attended church most of those years, but because he was a very private person, I wondered after his death about his salvation and if he was with the Lord.

One day in prayer, as I was praying in the Spirit, God allowed me to see into the supernatural. I saw my father in Heaven! He appeared as a young man about 35 or 40 years old. He had dark, almost black hair, but at his death it was completely gray. This assured me that he was with the Lord and enjoying his heavenly home!

Joy:

Just before my son-in-law, Steve, went home to be with the Lord, he and my daughter were kneeling in prayer when my daughter looked at him. She said he was glowing and looked beautiful.

Later, Steve was telling his grandma about praying that day and said that he was in a beautiful place, all light, and that he wanted to stay. They told him, "Not now; you have to go back."

A week later, Steve was killed at work. He had led a man to the Lord the night before and took him to be baptized....

Mae:

My father was in a wheelchair for several years before he died. He had lost one leg and the other one was bad. He was almost blind and almost completely deaf. He suffered from diabetes, high blood pressure, and heart trouble. He was a Christian all his life and brought us up to love the Lord and go to church.

A few nights after he died I had a dream. I saw him standing on a beautiful green hillside—well and healthy, smiling and happy. That same week, my sister had the same dream!

We no longer mourned for him, but were filled with peace and comfort over his death.

Teresa:

I lost my baby girl when I was seven months pregnant. I had asked God to let me know she was in His hands. About five years later, during praise and worship, I entered God's presence and saw my little girl with Jesus. She had long dark hair. She told me she was being taken care of and not to be afraid or worry. She said she loved me and would wait for me in Heaven. I was in such peace and contentment. Jesus spoke a few words to me and I released the emotions I had carried and now I have been able to deal with the loss. I know I will see her in Heaven.

Sandee:

I was expecting my third child, a son. This pregnancy had progressed rather uneventfully. At this point, I only had four weeks left until my due date.

Suddenly, I awoke in the middle of the night. I sat up in bed like I had been struck by a bolt of lightning. A flurry of movement was all around me. I saw two angels, one on either side of me. Then I saw my baby son. It was as if he had risen up and out of me, and the angels took him between the two of them. In a brilliance of soft, silvery light, they quickly ascended upwards, going right through the ceiling as if it didn't exist.

I sat there, peaceful yet dazed. My mind was grappling with the scene I had just witnessed. The next day I went to the doctor's office to confirm what I already knew. My son had died in the night.

Indeed, there was sadness in the family, but I could not grieve as one who had no hope. My son is in the Father's house, and I will be seeing him, as well as my oldest daughter Christy, very soon.

Lisa:

[Describing her near-death experience as a young woman]: I remember leaving here at an incredible speed through space, passing bright lights that appeared to be stars. I saw a light and knew I was going to Heaven and would see God. The only way to describe it was great joy and peace, but the joy was especially intense...then as the life came back into my body, I felt a great rush of air surging through my ribs....

A Pastor:

In my dream, [my pastor friend] came and showed me a bright crown he had received for his labors. He encouraged me to keep on with my church, standing firm through the trials and demands. His exact words were, "It is worth it." I awoke with tears of joy.

Ruby:

The Lord showed me a vision just before my mother died. There was a whole crowd of loved ones gathered as a welcoming party at something like a train station waiting for my mama to arrive. I recognized so many of them: my daddy, my daughter Patsy who had died at 24 from cancer, my mother-in-law, and so many others. They knew mama was coming and were planning a celebration. The Lord told me that God sends out a message throughout Heaven to all the loved ones saying what time to be there, and they prepare a celebration. This is done for each of His children when they get to Heaven—a welcoming party!

Pauline:

I was the speaker for a woman's retreat in Illinois when I had the dream. I was in an empty room. Suddenly my son Charles, who had been brutally murdered, appeared. He came through the wall and was suspended between the floor and the ceiling. He was of such ethereal beauty that I was speechless and breathless. His hands were outstretched; his face glowed with joy. In a flash he was gone, and I was wide awake...and comforted.

Mike:

I was engaged in praise and worship that April morning, and had put in a music tape into my small headset. About ten minutes later, my whole being became very light, and my spirit began to be lifted out of my body. At first, I was reluctant to go because of the strangeness of it. I still remember how awkward my body felt and looked to me as I was lifted.

Immediately I perceived I was in the presence of a tremendous assembly of people—such a celebration, I can't explain. There was such love that seemed to be flowing all around, and singing, praising, dancing, and musical instruments. There was such joy that I was in a type of ecstasy. I could have spent eternity right there and never wanted for more. Filled with joy unspeakable, I scanned my eyes over the celebrants. It was at that moment I saw Emily [the daughter of a friend]—or that she saw me. Actually, we saw each other. She was beautiful beyond description. She looked to be about 25 years old, yet with a lovely depth and maturity that no 25-year-old ever had. She had flowing, radiant hair, and peaceful, loving eyes. Those eyes—love shone from them and smote me, immediately causing me to cry, not like a baby cries, just crying because I couldn't take it in. She smiled at me and lifted her hands upward and forward, indicating the direction of everyone's attention. I knew she was directing my attention to the Person of Jesus Christ....

Madeline:

We [the Lord and I] started down through fields that were so beautiful; the grass felt like a thick carpet. There were beautiful flowers and trees. There was not one blade of dead grass, no dead flowers, no brown leaves on any tree....

A Heavenly Cloud of Witnesses

Maxine:

My grandmother really loved the Lord. She was always praising Him and telling others about Jesus. Long after she had passed on, I had an open vision of her one night during our worship service. She was dancing and praising God in Heaven even like I was doing on earth, and she said to me, "I love it! I love what I see, so keep it up!"

Paige:

After previously miscarrying twins due to a severe infection, I was told I would never again have children. After prayer for healing and receiving a prophetic word, along with my husband's encouragement, with much joy we conceived again. At almost the exact same number of weeks as before, the same problems reoccurred and the battle began again to deliver another set of twins. But we were determined...my husband Ralph battled constantly in the spirit realm, and I battled emotionally and physically, including a forced bedrest for five months. By the grace of God we delivered two small but healthy baby girls eight weeks early. Though sleep was rare for me after the delivery, I laid down one afternoon while both twins were asleep. I had a vision of myself walking through a field of flowers with my dad's arm wrapped about me. His voice and personality were crystal clear, which was a distinctive feature of this encounter since my father had gone home to be with the Lord years before when I was 18. He said how proud he was of me for walking through this pregnancy in faith, and that the heavenly reward would far outweigh even the blessing of having the girls. Then he spoke Hebrews 12:1 to me: "Therefore, since we have so great a cloud of witnesses surrounding us, let us also lay aside every encumbrance and the sin which so easily entangles us, and let us run with endurance the race that is set before us, fixing our eyes on Jesus."

The vision was quickly over, but I called Ralph and my mother right away, still shaking from its reality.

As I thought out loud to myself later, "Lord, I really don't understand this...why didn't YOU just tell me these words?" The internal response was immediate and clear: "Because I knew it would mean more to have your father tell you."

For I consider that the sufferings of this present time are not worthy to be compared with the glory which shall be revealed in us.

For the earnest expectation of the creation eagerly waits for the revealing of the sons of God.

For the creation was subjected to futility, not willingly, but because of Him who subjected it in hope;

because the creation itself also will be delivered from the bondage of corruption into the glorious liberty of the children of God.

For we know that the whole creation groans and labors with birth pangs together until now.

Not only that, but we also who have the firstfruits of the Spirit, even we ourselves groan within ourselves, eagerly waiting for the adoption, the redemption of our body.

For we were saved in this hope, but hope that is seen is not hope; for why does one still hope for what he sees?

But if we hope for what we do not see, we eagerly wait for it with perseverance.

Romans 8:18-25, New King James Version

Visit your local Christian bookstore
Where the Light always shines!
Destiny Image
This ad provided by Destiny Image Publishers, working in partnership with bookstores and distributors worldwide.